Paddling the
NORTHERN FOREST CANOE TRAIL

DAN TOBYNE *with* ERIC ALEXANDER

Down East Books
Camden, Maine, and Guilford, Connecticut

Rangeley, Maine.

Down East Books

An imprint of The Rowman & Littlefield Publishing Group, Inc.
4501 Forbes Blvd., Ste. 200
Lanham, MD 20706
www.rowman.com

Distributed by NATIONAL BOOK NETWORK

British Library Cataloguing in Publication Information available

Library of Congress Cataloging-in-Publication Data available

ISBN 978-1-60893-692-2 (paper : alk. paper)
ISBN 978-1-60893-693-9 (electronic)

∞™ The paper used in this publication meets the minimum requirements of American National Standard for Information Sciences—Permanence of Paper for Printed Library Materials, ANSI/NISO Z39.48-1992.

This book is dedicated to three people; my two kids Jared and Caitie; they are the glue that binds me, and my friend and former back seater, Brad Currier. When other people were running away, he stepped toward the noise; volunteering for the Army, then volunteering for Airborne before volunteering for Viet Nam, and finally for combat. His Purple Heart says it all, and I'm proud to call him my friend and brother. I hope he knows that even though his paddling is limited these days; I see him always, when I stare into the flame.

Contents

NORTHERN FOREST CANOE TRAIL
WWW.NORTHERNFORESTCANOETRAIL.ORG
Fort Kent
CANADA
Québec
MAINE
Vermont
Old Forge
New York
New
Hampshire
Northern Forest Canoe Trail

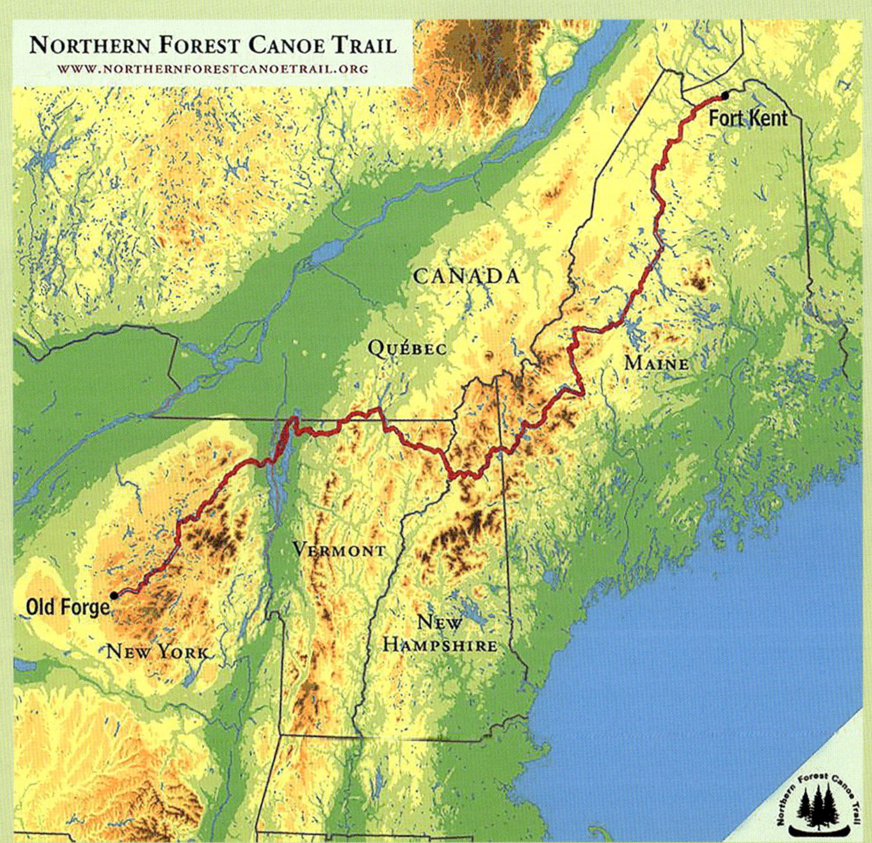

Early morning paddle on Chamberlain Lake in the Allagash.

There isn't a lot that's more agreeable to us than sitting in a canoe on a quiet pond or slow-moving river, with a slight breeze slowly nudging our bow before dying away, as if a silent hand is trying to guide us in some unknown direction. In the words of Wendell Berry:

> Always in big woods when you leave familiar ground and step off alone into a new place there will be, along with the feelings of curiosity and excitement, a little nagging dread—You are undertaking the first experience, not of the place, but of yourself in that place. It is an experience of our essential loneliness, for nobody can discover the world for anybody else. It is only after we have discovered it for ourselves that it becomes a common ground and a common bond, and we cease to be alone.

Wendell was talking about hiking off into the big wild; we think the philosophy fits paddling off into the great outdoors as well.

Introduction

No wind, a low sun, and cool air; a quiet morning paddle on a mirror lake where the only sound is the dipping of one's paddle and the low whoosh of the canoe as it breaks the fathomless plain; this is nature in all its glory.

For us it's never been about the end result but always about the journey, and as we've grown older, it's moments like this that awaken our dormant soul. If you want to explore your physical self, be a thru-paddler, and test your metal against the elements. If you want to explore the trail, the world, and, more importantly, your inner self, be a section paddler. For the record, Eric and I might not even be considered section paddlers, we're more like turtles; we move slowly, take in everything we can, and hardly ever paddle in a straight line, even when it's part of the plan. For us an erratic zigzag journey is the best way to explore the world around us, allowing us to stop and look things over, to wander and absorb things we might have missed had we been paddling to meet benchmarks and schedules. Nix on the badges. We're inveterate wanderers who believe the whole is more than the sum of its parts, and only through exploring can we understand how we fit in to the world we see around us. Thoreau wrote the following in *Walden* and we wholeheartedly agree:

> We need the tonic of wildness. . . . At the same time that we are earnest to explore and learn all things, we require that all things be mysterious and unexplorable, that land and sea be indefinitely wild, unsurveyed and unfathomed by us because unfathomable. We can never have enough of nature.

We spent the better part of two summers, a spring, and two falls working on this book and it's an adventure we'll appreciate for the rest of our lives. Our experiences at times were visceral and "in your face," and we loved it, but the true appreciation of what we experienced will come at some point down the road, because one truth about learning is written in stone. The learning comes later, and only by reflection can we truly grasp and absorb what we experience.

We'll be back next year and the year after that; we didn't paddle every inch nor could we, so there's more to do. At some lakes, we simply stood on the shore and thought: Holy crap, look at how big those waves are, and how hard the wind blew in our face. At other times, we stared in disbelief at all the boulders and wondered where the water had gone. As seasoned wanderers, we have a few simple rules, and safety trumps excitement the same way experience guides inexperience.

Double rainbow over Greenville Maine on Moosehead Lake.

Wants and needs dictate how you approach an adventure like this one, but nature sets the parameters, and it plays no favorites, is unyielding, and if you don't respect its power it will exact a heavy price. Nature doesn't feel bad for you if things go wrong, nor does it try to teach you any lessons, so it's imperative as a participant to respect its power and learn from your mistakes.

The other issue for us while working on this project was the difficulty of balancing our inveterate love of the out of doors with our workload. There were times when we did something and then had to do it again because like any hunter, we as photographers were searching for a special place, a special mood, a special kind of lighting or other factor to get the "picture." More than once Eric heard me say, "This is it." or "This isn't it. Can we drive back here tomorrow morning? It's only 85 miles." Mood is also an important component for us to communicate successfully as photographers, and if we've done our job, the pictures we take speak as much or more than the words we write. A good photograph pulls the viewer in and draws on his or her emotions. A good photograph can say it all.

Often, when returning from a trip filled with clouds and rain, people would tell us how sorry they were about all the "bad" weather we'd encountered. We'd just smile and say to ourselves; "No, no, no, that's exactly what we needed and wanted, and yes the rain may have made it hard, and we may have been miserable at times, but it's exactly what we needed to get the kind of photography we were searching for."

There's also a gift we receive when we come to terms with tough situations—when we embrace the misery. In the worst of times, and we've had some hard times, I'd mention to Eric with a smirk that we might be in the "moment." Standing in water and soaked to the bone—wet, tired, sore, and smelling like dead animals, having our mental toughness tested by an incessant army of black flies, or just plain chilled to the bone with no hope of finding dry clothes, are all potential moments to remember. It's the memory to think about after Thanksgiving dinner when others have loosened their belts and trying to nap, watching some football game they aren't really interested in, or trying to figure out why they didn't take Friday off. It's the moment we hope to think back on and reflect; and whatever the misery, just the mention of that possibility allows us to laugh together, knowing that on the third Thursday in November we have a present to mentally unwrap, one that will make us smile all over again.

The trail covers approximately 740 miles and includes 22 streams and rivers, 58 lakes and ponds, and 53 miles of portaging divided among 63 "carries," but unless you plan on canoeing in a straight line from Old Forge to Fort Kent, you're going to paddle more than 740 miles and portage more than 53 miles. Many rivers and streams become unnavigable during dry conditions and require extra portaging. Wet conditions can also change the narrative, sometimes creating more portaging "opportunities," sometimes less, depending on what portion of the trail you're paddling.

We began our adventure on a warm spring day, setting out from a small beach next to the dam in the hamlet of Old Forge in the Adirondacks, a stone's throw from the Northern Forest Canoe Trail (NFCT) kiosk that marks the trail's western terminus; and we ended our adventure on a wet September afternoon eighteen months later at a boat launch in a small park just below the Fort Kent Blockhouse. We still aren't quite sure how we missed the Fort Kent NFCT kiosk, nor do we care. At the time it was a big deal, and we ran around looking for our grail, convinced we needed a picture of us in front of it—a closure shot for the book—until it dawned on us that our trip, as in life, isn't about the beginning nor is it about the end. It's really about everything in the middle, and we'd done a pretty good job covering all that stuff in the middle at least this time around, so we saddled up and headed off in search of dry clothes as new thoughts began to circle around in our heads about what might be in store for us next year.

There are also a few gifts you can receive if you spend enough time in the outdoors; the sound of a loon calling its mate in the early evening darkness, the view of a morning sun after a rainstorm, the crisp snap in the air on a fall morning, and if you're lucky enough to know how to build one, and you're open to the power of memory, one of the best-kept secrets of all, the mystical experience of a campfire.

CAMPFIRE

I sometimes receive a text from a friend and all it says is; "I need a campfire," a phrase that means a lot more than its four words. It's code for; get me off if only for a while, this high-speed elevator with its constant questions, problems, and noise, it's never-ending buzz and hundred-mile-an-hour pace, its brain pulverizing, stress inducing roller coaster. Slow me down so I can think. Slow me down so I can reflect. Slow me down so I can relax. Slow me down so I can find the wisdom in my life that's been drowned out by everything else. Help! I need to clear the mechanism. And a campfire has the power to do that!

Fire symbolizes the essence of our human existence, it is mystical and magic, it is an incubator of life and the curator of our spiritual soul. Fire is a transformational event both physically through the flame and mystically through our minds. It's a symbol of wisdom, of purity and spiritual energy, and it holds the power to transfix us. It's hypnotic and magic, and part of its allure is the realization, that it can take us to another place; a place of reflection, a place with the ability to deafen the background noise and rejuvenate the soul. The most oft-used phrase spoken when people are staring into a campfire is; "Do you remember when. . . . "

The place that fire brings me to, allows me as a participant, to visit and revisit past experiences. It reignites emotions in me and transports me to places I've long forgotten or only remembered in objective terms. It plays with my senses and sparks long forgotten memories. If you stare into a campfire long enough, its hypnotic power sometimes allows you to reach an alternate level of

human consciousness, a dream state that taps into memory, sometimes allowing us to understand our personal history by sensitizing us to long hidden thoughts and dreams. It often opens all of this up to me and bathes me in the reality of all that is, all that was, and all that will ever be.

A campfire burns in a circle without sides, without a front or a back, and is a release of physical and spiritual energy that dances in the night sky sometimes taking us along for the ride. Fire is one of the four elements of life; earth, wind, and water being the others. A fire's transformative power can place me back in my grandfather's yard

watching carp swimming in his backyard fishpond. I'm transported back into my grandfather's presence; I can see him, feel him, and smell him, as he tells me how to feed the fish. I can be thirteen again and riding my bike on that hot summer day when I wiped out at the end of the street, skinning my arms, legs and face. The memory is so vivid I wince as though this long-ago event just happened. I can return to the scene of previous adventures and have sometimes accidently called a new friend, by an old friend's name because memories have been rekindled, past experiences reignited. My father, my long-lost friends and family, all roll back into reality and are present as a vision in that moment. I feel the magic of past campfires; flames dancing, wisps of smoke rolling skyward as the air feeds the flames. I feel as though I am not alone in my dreams, but others are close by.

Secrets are shared around a campfire because those who've experienced the magic understand it's okay to verbalize things, things we might never tell anyone, any other time. The trance of the glowing flame is powerful medicine.

THINGS TO KNOW BEFORE YOU GO

CREATING A PACKING LIST

It's one thing to plan your trip, but it's another to prepare and pack for it, and how and what you pack will determine how enjoyable your experience will be. Before you go, you'll need to organize and pack three basic types of equipment; paddling gear, camping gear, and personal gear, and it all needs to be organized and accounted for before you step off into the wild. These are what our lists look like.

PACKS, BAGS, AND SOMETIMES BOXES

A trip on the water involves the possibility that everything you pack will at some point get wet, making the bags, packs, and containers you choose to take, of special importance. You will also need to balance two competing requirements when packing: keeping things dry and your ability to carry your gear around unnavigable sections of the trail—portaging as it's called, from one place to another.

I own a large seventies era Kelty Backpack with an external frame that's the best pack I've ever owned, but it's not a pack I usually bring on a canoe trip. It's too rigid, the

Our canoe on the Allagash loaded with gear; three drybags with camera gear in the bow, camera in waterproof case on the seat along with one-man tent; center section holds my day pack, Eric's black canoe pack, and my Kelty backpack; aft section contains our yellow wannigan, waterproof drone pack, map case, and 5-gallon waterproof bucket.

external frame is problematic because it doesn't pack well in a canoe, and it's almost impossible to access when secured for water travel. Instead, Eric and I each bring two packs; a small daypack stocked with items we may need to access while canoeing, and a large frameless pack commonly referred to as a canoe pack. Canoe packs come in a variety of sizes from 45 to 120 liters. We prefer one that ranges between 80 and 100. Canoe packs are not waterproof, and you'll need to double bag your gear with trash bags; If you don't trust that method, you'll need to use drybags. Drybags come in a variety of sizes but be careful how many you bring because they're usually bulky, don't pack well, and although some come with pack straps, you'll need to decide how many portaging trips you're willing to make to move your gear from one point to another. I use heavy duty drybags for my camera gear and make sure when I seal them, I leave a good amount of air in the bag. I also wrap the cameras in towels for protection. It makes for a bulky mess at times, but at least the bags will float if they go overboard. If we're particularly concerned about our cameras, we sometimes pack them in a large Pelican case but only include that when we know we won't be portaging any great distance. When you portage with that kind of case, it's problematic; they're large, very heavy by design and awkward to carry, besides that; you look like a door-to-door salesman who wandered off and got lost in the woods. When we take along our drone, we pack it in a heavy-duty waterproof hard-box and place that case into a waterproof backpack; it's the one piece of camera equipment not covered by our insurance policy, so we take extra precautions. We like to use lightweight compression bags for things like clothing, sleeping bags, and anything else compressible. When we know we'll be portaging on a trip, we pack as much equipment and gear as possible in our canoe packs; the less upside-down canoeing between waterbodies the better.

On any canoe trip lasting more than two days we bring a wannigan; a storage box and traditional piece of canoeing equipment, its name, derived from the Ojibwa word *waanikaan*, means "storage pit," its purpose is to carry all those hard to pack items needed on a trip. Traditionally wannigans were constructed of wood and fancy ones would even conform to the canoe's curves. Our wannigan is plastic with a sealable lid.

Many have a tumpline—a strap allowing the carrier to use his head to support most of the weight. Our box doesn't have a tumpline; my neck having suffered enough abuse over the years, I don't need to contribute to the damage by carrying a 30-pound box around by my head. I'd be more than happy to install a tumpline if I could get Eric to carry it, but he keeps telling me his mother didn't raise any fools, so we have lines attached to both sides of the box allowing us to carry the box with a pole or do a simple two-man carry. Sometimes a wannigan will be fitted out with straps allowing the use of a pack platform to aid in carrying with or without a tumpline.

CANOES AND KAYAKS

You'll need a boat! The general rule is a canoe or kayak, although some of the trail can be visited in almost anything that will float. We used several canoes depending on how much gear we needed to take, what type of paddling we thought we'd encounter, and how long we expected to be on the water. Our number one is a 16-foot Old Town Discovery 169. The Old Town is a very good river canoe, tracks well in whitewater and is a workhorse when it comes to the amount of gear it can hold. We also used a Mad River 14-foot Adventure canoe. This canoe tracks well because of its modified keel and we used it mostly for day tripping because of its limited weight carrying capacity.

We like kayaking as much as we love canoeing and the best kayak for our purposes is a fishing kayak because of its stability. We use 10-foot polyethylene kayaks with a carrying capacity of 355 pounds; they're great for lakes and rivers, track well in rough water, is a great camping kayak, and although not very good for running heavy whitewater, they're just what we need. Our boats have a double-chined hull and a wide cockpit for storing gear that needs to be accessible, as well as a dashboard for securing all the items we want close—insect repellent, our cell phone in a waterproof case, sunglasses, and sunscreen, any number of items you wouldn't want rolling around in the bottom of the boat.

When packing a canoe, you can bring along a lot of equipment and we sometimes bring way too much gear. When we pack for a kayaking trip, we don't skimp on safety equipment but everything else is up for discussion and the overarching question we ask ourselves is; what can we live without? Our Old Town canoe can handle about 600 pounds of extra gear and that's a lot for a canoe trip. Our kayaks on the other hand can handle about 100 pounds extra for each boat. That's still a lot, but the real issue with packing a kayak is not the amount of weight you can carry but the amount of space you have. Ours kayaks have only enough room in the two internal compartments for camping gear requiring most of our camera gear to be strapped to the boat's deck, leaving little room for anything else.

Author's kayak.

PADDLES

Don't laugh, I've seen people pack everything imaginable for a trip and forget to bring their paddles. They're like orphans that some people don't pay attention to until it's time to launch their vessel, so make sure you have them on your checklist and pack them before you leave home.

Canoe paddles come in various different materials; wood, plastic, or composite, different shapes; fat, skinny, bent or straight; and different sizes; long, short, or in between, so choosing the correct paddle depends a little on preference, and a lot on what kind of canoe you own and how you go about paddling. The length of your torso and arms, the distance from your shoulder to the surface of the water, what kind of canoe or kayak you're using, and whether you canoe sitting or kneeling, are all factors when choosing the correct paddle length. There are several scientific measurements you can use to determine the best length. Our method for determining how long our paddles should be however is decidedly unscientific. When in the stern we use a straight paddle that measures from the ground to our eyes, and when paddling from the bow, we use a paddle that measures to our chin. When I'm in the stern and splashing a little on the front sweep, the paddle is probably too long. When this occurs, I kneel upright pressing my thighs against the cross-rail to add a little height, which is my most comfortable paddling position.

Paddles also break, fall overboard, get lost during a capsizing, and sometimes are misplaced, so you should always bring a spare one, maybe two, and have them securely strapped in place. There's no sense losing all your paddles if you roll your boat.

If you're in a kayak, your paddle options are limited. The only real concern besides what type of material your paddle is made of—you can go with wood, plastic, or fiberglass, is the length of the paddle. Our Kayaks are wide, and we use a longer paddle than usual. I still ship water with a longer paddle, but I've come to expect that. Ours have a graphite shaft and break down for ease of storage; something you can't do if you opt for one made of wood. We also have cockpit skirts; not the wearable kind but ones we can keep on the kayak when it's not in the water, allowing us to keep our gear in the kayak at the end of the day, it also keeps rain and critters out when parked at our campsite.

Additionally the cover guards against unwanted guests like spiders, and field mice taking up residence when the boats are stored for the winter or between trips; there's nothing more uncomfortable than a big spider crawling up your leg while you're in the middle of a paddle downriver unless of course it's a field mouse or a snake.

PFD

A PFD is a life safety device and a survival aid for those of us who enjoy adventure activities around water. The normal PFD for canoeing and kayaking is a Standard Type III vest. It's filled with foam or other floatable material, and if you land in the water wearing a properly fitted one, it does all the work of keeping you afloat. The drawbacks of a standard vest are its propensity to be hot and bulky. As an alternative you can wear an inflatable Type III PFD and there are two types; ones that automatically fill up with air when they come in contact with the water, and others that are activated when the wearer pulls a cord. I'm not a fan of inflatables, because they're high maintenance, and obsolete if ripped or punctured; not something I want to rely on in the backcountry.

The vests we wear have lots of pockets and as photographers who carry a lot of gear, having pockets is a necessity. We also pocket a lot of items we might need in an emergency and carry a canoe knife unobtrusively attached to a horizontal strap; readily available in the event of an emergency. The concern we need to pay attention to is buoyancy. Vests need to support the added weight a wearer carries if he/she ends up in the water.

Adult vests are sized by chest size while children's vests are sized by weight, and a standard vest needs to pass the pull test to ensure it's properly fitted. Put the vest on, zip it up, secure all the straps to ensure snugness and then have someone pull the vest upward from behind at the shoulders. The job of a vest is to keep your nose and mouth above the water; if the vest rides up past your chin, it's too big. You should also make sure the vest fits with the clothing you'll be wearing while canoeing, which might be very different from what you have on in a store when shopping.

If you're taking young children or a weak swimmer along, you might consider having them wear a Type I vest. Although a properly fitted Type III PFD will keep a person buoyant, it requires the wearer to place themselves face up. A Type I vest is the most buoyant type of vest on the market and will usually automatically turn a person into a face up position.

Our PFDs are also the closest thing we have, to what you might call a survival kit. It isn't our intention to be very far from our canoe or kayaks, we don't usually go hiking off after a day on the water, but since we aren't actually tied to our vessel, there's always the chance we might find ourselves without a boat, and if we were to lose our gear and transportation, we would hopefully still have our life vests so we try to not store them in our boats. When not wearing our vests, we store them high and dry—or wet, depending on the weather, and easily accessible at our campsite.

PAINTERS

A painter is a line usually used to secure a boat, and your boat should have one on the bow and another attached at the stern. When walking a canoe or kayak around dangerous whitewater these lines are essential to stabilize the boat. It's also something to grab if you fall overboard or capsize.

THROW BAG

A throw bag is used to rescue someone who's gone overboard and needs help. Learning how to throw this kind of line when trying to save someone isn't the smartest way to learn how to use one. You should practice with the line before you go on a trip. Learning the throwing technique takes practice; you should also practice coiling it properly. Throwing the bag releases the floating line, and if you're a good aim and have taken the time to practice with it, you have a chance of being successful on the first try. The goal is to hit the person in the water with the bag allowing them to grab hold and be pulled to safety so throw it underhand and aim for the person's head, that's the best chance they'll have to grab the line. One of the most important steps for being successful with this safety tool whether using it from your boat or from shore, is making sure you tie the other end to something, otherwise your friend and the rescue line will both end up floating downriver.

BAILER

Some of our gear are like socks in the laundry. Even though we pack it all in the truck, some of it always goes missing and our bailer is one of those items so our solution for this errant piece of equipment is decidedly homemade and on the cheap. We cut the bottom off an empty one-gallon bleach bottle and we're ready to bail. Bleach bottles seem to work the best because of their thickness. We've seen the recommendations to bring a sponge along to remove the hard to get water in the bottom of our vessel and we used to bring one but have stopped doing that because wet sponges that travel from one place to another and tend to stay wet after everything else has dried out, often assists invasive species to move from one body of water to another. Everyone these days seem to be making a big deal out of inspecting boats for invasive species before launching onto a waterway, but we often don't think about the sponge we used to clean the canoe, and its ability to function as a great transport mechanism for unwanted, intrusive species. Bailer yes, sponge no.

PORTAGE WHEELS

Exploring the route of the Northern Forest Canoe Trail requires portaging, sometimes called land paddling. The NFTC has 62 portages totaling 55-plus miles of walking with a canoe or kayak so any assist you can give your shoulders is a great help. We have a set of portage wheels that help in two different ways. We can wheel the canoe and at the same time, keep some of our gear in place, reducing the number of back-and-forth trips required to move everything from one water source to another. We prefer hard wheels to inflatable ones because we don't want to bring along even more gear for fixing flats.

MAPS, GUIDEBOOKS, AND COMPASS

The Northern Forest Canoe Trail is mapped out across 13 special maps and you might think there's no need to bring a compass along but that's not true. A compass is a valuable tool and you should always bring one with you when off the beaten path. You should consider bringing along a topographic map of the area. Compasses and maps also function a lot like first aid kits. No matter how good they are, they're useless if you don't know how to use them and being lost in the woods isn't the time to try to learn.

We carry mountaineering compasses that account for declination. Declination is the difference between true north and magnetic north and it's different depending on your location. In the eastern United States declination runs anywhere from -15 to -20

degrees in New England, to 0 degrees in Florida. For the Northeast United States and Eastern Canada declination is about -15 degrees of true north.

All this discussion about compass readings, declination, and maps is because it's easy to become disoriented when on the water or in the woods and without a fixed-point of reference, the ability to become even more disoriented is a distinct possibility. "Is this the cove, or is that the cove?" "Should we go up this bend in the river?" "Should we get out and walk around?" And the ultimate question; "Where are we"? A wrong answer to any of these questions has the potential to get you lost and being lost without the tools to get yourself unlost is a very bad feeling, not to mention a potentially danger-ous situation. Of course, if you don't know how to use a compass it's just another use-less piece of equipment you packed, so like first aid kits, we recommend you develop some fundamental skills.

CAMPING GEAR

SLEEPING BAG AND PAD

Sleeping bags are a personal preference. They come in different sizes and shapes, designed for different seasons and temperatures, are adjustable, and have various types of insulation or "fill." Down bags are probably the most lightweight but also the most expensive, and they have drawbacks that other bags don't have. When a down bag becomes wet, it loses most if not all its insulating value, and hey, the NFCT is a water trail so it's not just inclement weather you need to worry about when it comes to how wet your gear might become. They're also a little harder to clean and require more TLC than synthetic-filled bags.

There are bags on the market for family camping that shouldn't be considered as canoe trail bags. They look like big quilts, can be zipped together to create two-person bags and are usually filled with insulation material that doesn't compress well, if at all. They absorb water, become very heavy when wet and are probably unusable in anything but a dry state.

The third option and our choice are synthetically filled bags. Polyester filled bags are heavier than down, although not by much. They also lose insulating value every time they're stuffed in a sack, but I've had mine for twelve years and it still seems to work okay. We're tough on our equipment and these bags can take a lot of abuse. Unlike down, polyester retains an insulating value when wet, which is a huge plus. If we rip them, we fix them with duct tape, if they get dirty, we throw them in the washer and dryer. Poly fill bags contain either short-staple or continuous filament fill. Short staple feels softer and more like down, but the fill can bunch up—like down, creating cold spots. Continuous filament is stiffer and a little bulkier, but the insulation stays in place.

We each own two bags; a 30-degree modified mummy with a little extra wiggle room, and a zero-degree mummy for maximum warmth. Eric also owns a 50-degree bag, but to me it looks more like a blanket someone stitched up and tried to pass off as a sleeping bag. Too each his own.

Our choice of fill is an easy one. We prefer a continuous filament, modified mummy, polyester fill bag. They cost less, take a lot of abuse, and function under conditions, other bags can't. Personally, I pay no attention to my sleeping bag until I get in it and forget about it once I get out of it. I often forget to take it out of its stuff sack when I'm not using it and after 12-years of use, or maybe I should say abuse, it still doing its job. Besides, when camping with a bag that doesn't seem to keep you warm anymore and probably needs to be retired, there's a simple solution while you're in the field. Put more clothes on especially a hat before you crawl in.

TENTS

The three most important requirements for a tent are; waterproof floor, a fine mesh screen—fine enough to keep no-see-ums out, and a rain fly. We have a number of tents for different occasions; a six-person Coleman tent for those times we stay in a campground, a two-man twenty-year-old Timberline mountain tent for camping along the trail, and two single person solo tents for those times along the trail where we know it's going to be tight for setting up camp. We tried bivy sacks but gave them the thumbs down. In warm weather it felt like we'd been buried alive. We also have hammocks although in rainy weather it's problematic to keep some things dry since there's very limited space in a hammock to store gear, and the fly basically protects the inhabitant and not much else.

The floor space for our two-man gives us roughly 5 x 7 feet of floor space allowing each of us about 30 inches in width. The peak height is 3 ft 6 in., so there's no standing

One-man mountain tent.

up in this tent and really, it's only used for sleeping. Our six-person tent is roomy compared to our other sleeping options. The height is over six feet allowing us to stand up, and it's roomy enough to allow us to use cots. This is living in luxury compared to our other options and it's our choice when staying in a campground. The versatility of the one person tents gives us the ability to set up camp for the night almost any place; we can also set them up when sleeping in a lean-to or Adirondack shelter giving us each a bug free space. If necessary, we can also sleep right next to our kayaks or canoe. When weight is a concern, and it usually is when we're traveling in kayaks, we opt for hammocks or our solo tents, each weigh less than 3 lbs.

HATCHET AND SAW

We don't bring an ax; they're too big for a canoe trip and doesn't make the packing list for a kayaking trip, were the philosophy is "What can we live without." We opt for hatchets and have two models. We pack a Fiskars hatchet with plastic locking case on our canoe trips, it does the job, which is mostly firewood related, and we bring a smaller short-handle hatchet on trips when kayaking. The smaller hatchet is lighter and more compact although not as safe as a hatchet with a more traditional-length handle. We sometimes bring a saw along but only consider foldable models for two reasons; they pack better, and they're safer to transport. We like the folding Sven backpacking saw because the blade is hidden when the saw is broken down.

TARP

Don't forget to bring a tarp; its importance is right up there with toilet paper. We forgot ours on our trip to the upper Allagash and paid a heavy price. We carry a tarp to shed water. We set it up to stay out of the rain at our campsite and we cover our gear with it when necessary. We don't place a tarp on the ground before we set up our tent. We've read the information about extending the life of a tent's floor by placing a tarp under it, but we aren't fans of that. Tarps under a tent, even these new footprint tarps that companies have started selling tend to allow water to be trapped between the two layers and sleeping on a water sandwich is never a good idea. Besides, if our tent's bottom is in the final days of its life because of abrasion and wear-and-tear, so are most of the other components, and it's time to buy a new tent. Our Timberline two-man is 20 years old, has seen extensive use including the summit of twelve 4,000-footers (mountains), has never had a tarp placed under it, and is still going strong.

When you forget your tarp, there's no place to run and no place to hide. You just have to unfortunately, embrace the wetness.

FIRST AID KIT

A first aid kit is an essential item for any trip into the wild, and it's a piece of equipment you hope you never need to use, but when and if you do, everyone venturing out on an adventure should have some knowledge or how to treat injuries and at least one person should have a more extensive knowledge of how to deal with wilderness trauma. Reading the cheat sheet that comes with most kits while trying to administer first aid is ill conceived; time is the one thing you don't want to run out of during an emergency.

There are many kits on the market today covering all types of needs. There are small individual first aid packets that are good for simple needs, and kits for extended trips into the backcountry. We pack two types; a small individual kit for common medical concerns like; blisters, small cuts, splinters, headaches and the like, and a larger first aid kits stashed away that we hope we never need to pull out but it's there and ready if we need it. We both carry our individual kits in one of our PFD pockets or in our day pack for ease of access. We keep them in a waterproof ziplock bag for added protection and since most kits don't have everything we like to see

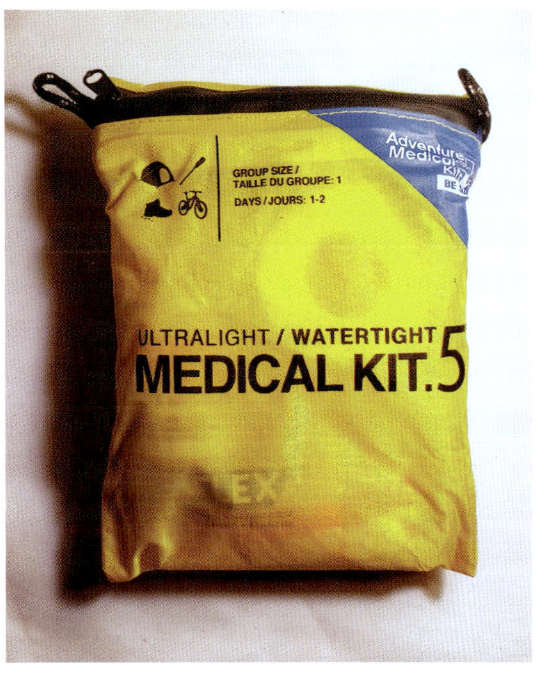

Individual waterproof first aid kit that's normally carried in our PFD.

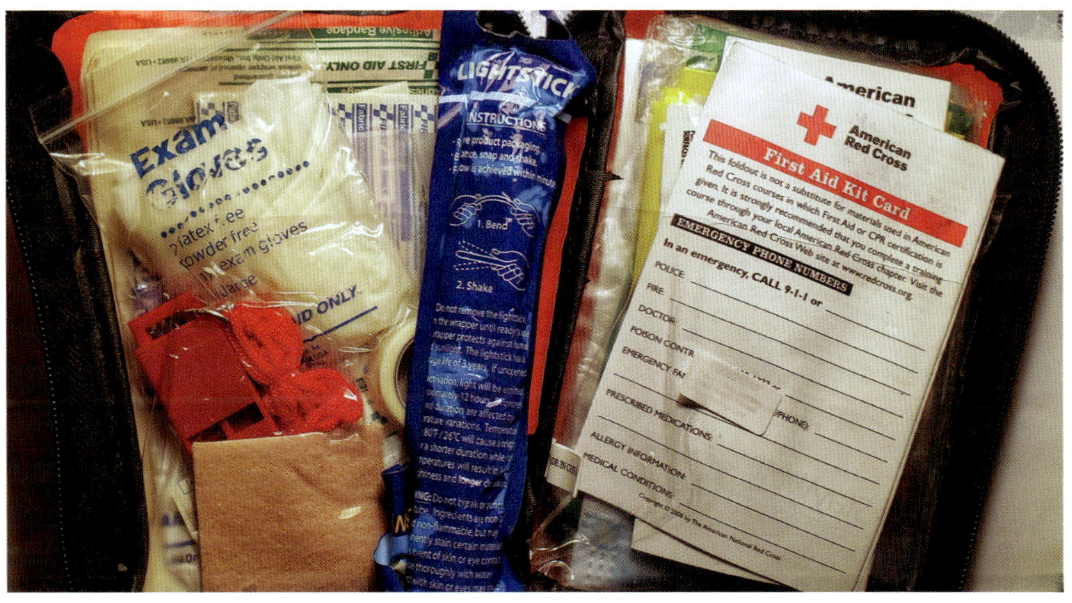

in a small kit, we both add a few additional items. I add heavy-duty fabric band-aids including ones designed for the knuckles and fingertips, extra aspirin tablets, ibuprofen tablets, and Benadryl, along with a small bottle of Superglue—best liquid bandage on the market, for cuts and cracks.

We've used many of the larger kits sold on the market, but find they always seem to have things included that we don't need, and items we believe essential often left out, so we prefer to organize our own kits.

Our kits include the following items:

- Gauze, usually 2½ x 2½ sterile dressing and a roll
- Band aids–We prefer cloth band aids. They stay in place even when wet.
- Small bar of soap
- Elastic bandage; 3 inch and 4 inch
- Tape; we pack two types waterproof tape and a roll of cloth athletic tape.
- Butterfly bandages–Butterfly bandages are good for closing cuts and lacerations especially those that would probably require stitches. You can also use medical tape to make a butterfly but recently we've discovered Spyroflex dressing for closing lacerations.
- Spenco 2nd Skin Aquaheal hydrogel bandages
- Mole skin for blisters
- Aspirin
- Ibuprofen tablets 200mg
- Benadryl
- Maximum strength triple-antibiotic ointment
- Pramoxine for temporarily relieve itching and pain caused by skin irritation cause by burns, scrapes, sunburn, insect bites, or rashes from poison ivy, poison oak, or poison sumac.
- New Skin liquid bandage–works great for cracks and cuts on the hands–I use Super Glue.
- Universal "oll" splint: 4.5" x 36" and self-adhesive gauze–This type of splint is customizable, and pliable enough to be cut to length and molded to all sorts of shapes, depending on the injury. It's also reusable.
- Trauma scissors
- Tick extractor tool: Looks like a small spoon with a v-notch cutout.
- Small Swiss Army Knife, the ones with the toothpick and tweezers.

We don't place prescription medication in our first aid kits. We pack those in our day packs or toilet kits, fitted into a waterproof container for safe carrying. We also don't place insect repellent or Chapstick in our kit. Each of us carries our own supply for use when needed. It's not a good idea to be constantly digging around in emergency equipment for items better carried on our person. We prefer to keep our first aid kit untouched and ready for use when needed.

INSECT REPELLANT

Anyone outside during black fly or mosquito season knows the importance of carrying insect repellant, and a repellant that works can make all the difference between a good experience and a miserable one. There are lots of insect repellants on the market and many contain DEET as the active ingredient. We've used those repellants and will probably use them again, but anything that melts the face of my watch and the sleeve of my jacket makes me think twice no matter what the experts say. In addition, we have the added concern it might melt some parts of our camera gear and that would be a real problem. We've used Wildwood, an all-natural product made in Saranac Lake, New York and if you'd like to try it, Google "Carpé Insectae," we've also had good success with White Mountain; a DEET free insect repellent produced in Merrimac, New Hampshire that's recommended to protect against; midges, black flies and no-see-ums, but our favorite and we believe most effective, is Obie Sherer's original Ole Time Woodsman Fly Dope, bottled in Maine since 1910. If you're lucky enough to get your hands on some, you'll realize how good it is; you'll also never forget the smell.

Obie believed insects like black flies and mosquitoes can't actually be repelled but it is possible to block their ability to detect carbon dioxide that we expel, and that's the secret behind his "Ole Time" Woodsman Fly Dope.

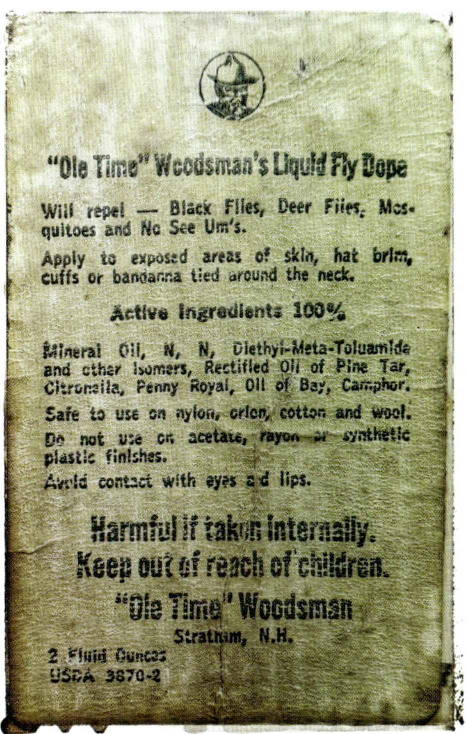

1976 label for Obie Sherer's original Ole Time Woodsman Fly Dope.

PERSONAL GEAR

Personal gear includes anything you'd pack for a trip that doesn't fall under the camping or canoeing category. There is some overlap which is fine just remember you need it, and make sure you pack it.

- Toilet paper
- Knife
- Individual first aid kit
- Canteen
- Mess kit (this is for eating; cup/spoon/plate/etc.)

- Flashlight
- Backpack
- Camera
- Clothing

TOILET KIT

Everyone should have their own personal toilet kit where they keep their toothbrush, toothpaste, soap (biodegradable), personal medications, and anything else they're accustomed to carrying when away on a trip. We pack prescription medication in our toilet kits. We don't want to dig through our first aid kit every day—which should be tucked away for an emergency, and personal prescriptions are just that, personal. Anything you do place in your toilet kit should be carried in a waterproof container or bag to prevent water damage.

TOILET PAPER

We're mentioning toilet paper again because it's that important. You might be able to find the outhouse, there are many along the trail, but don't expect to find toilet paper, make sure you pack your own supply because the substitutes for a lack of TP are unpleasant. We carry two kinds; regular toilet paper for use in an outhouse and marine TP if we need to dig a hole in the woods, the latter tends to fall apart if wet so you want to take extra precautions making sure it doesn't get damp, if it does you'll end up with something less than useful. If you find yourself without an outhouse, you'll need to perform what's known as cat-holing. You dig a hole about six inches deep and when done cover the hole which should also contain any toilet paper you used. Less than 6 inches and the waste may become exposed before decomposition. Too deep and it hinders decomposition.

KNIFE

You should carry a pocket-knife; we always do. It's an indispensable tool when in the woods. You should also carry a canoe knife that's accessible when you're on the water. There may be a time when you need quick access to a knife to cut your way out of a snag, strainer or tangled line on a river. We prefer a Morakniv knife because of their excellent Swedish carbon steel and their price—around $20. The two we prefer include a plastic sheath that allows us to keep the knife clipped to our PFD for easy access in an emergency. We don't cut cheese with it or use it to whittle. Its sole purpose is to be ready to assist us if needed. The two models we like are the Companion, and the Floating Serrated. The Morakniv Companion Knife is a stainless steel, utility knife sheathed with a plastic belt clip which keeps it firmly attached to our life jacket, it's easy to reach but out of the way and unobtrusive. It has a 4.1" drop-point stainless steel blade. The handle is made of thermoplastic elastomers (TPEs)—generally used in place of traditional rubbers these days, and the plastic sheath prevents us from accidentally stabbing ourselves during strenuous activities. Its overall length is 8.5 in. and the 4.1-in. blade has a thickness of 0.1 in.—not too thick, not too thin.

The other knife we like is the Morakniv Floating Serrated Knife It's thin (0.078 in.) and has a serrated blade that can easily chew through rope, and other materials. Its overall length at 9.25 in. makes it slightly longer than the Companion, and its shorter 3.7-in. blade with a rounded tip helps prevent

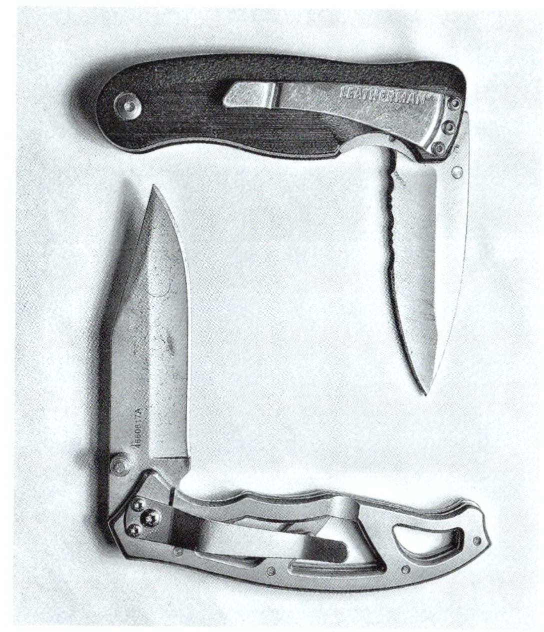

Swedish Morakniv knife, our standard canoe knife.

accidental punctures at chaotic moments. Unlike the Companion knife, this one floats, which combined with its orange high-visibility sheath makes it a better choice in some situations.

The third knife we bring on trips is a small Swiss Army knife—the one that comes with a toothpick and tweezers. We place it in our first aid kit for use if needed.

CANTEEN

We're surrounded by water on a water trail but very few water sources even in the wild are safe to drink without some form of purification. We recommend bringing along two canteens when out on the water. Canoeing like other strenuous activities burns calories, and dehydration is always a concern in warm weather especially when wearing a standard PFD. We bring Nalgene 32-ounce bottles which we pair with an Olicamp stainless steel cup. The cup slides on to the bottom of the bottle and doubles as a coffee and measuring cup; its measuring capability is important when you're main cooking style is rehydrating dehydrated food. We also carry a 5-gallon water jug when weight isn't an issue.

If you need to purify water while on a trip, there are a few different ways to do this. Boiling is the safest and best method. The CDC recommends boiling water for one minute. At that point bacteria, and parasites present in the water are neutralized. You can also, use a filter. Personal straw-like water systems exist on the market. They do a good job of eliminating bacteria, parasites, and microplastics but only work if the filter is kept clean. Another method is chemical treatment; halazone tablets, iodine, chlorine dioxide, and sodium hypochlorite all work well.

MESS KIT

You'll need a mess kit; we pack two, but our usual cooking method is boiling water and if we need to, we can function with just a coffee pot. We also don't bring many cooking utensils, because our usual diet consists of evaporated or freeze-dried food that comes in a bag, and a spoon is all that's required. If we share, we use our trusty coffee cups that also doubles as a measuring cup. We aren't diehard minimalists and do bring more than just a spoon and cup. We bring a plastic coffee press, a World War II era mess kit consisting of a pan with a folding handle and a plate, and a new age set of nesting pots with a removable handle and lids. When not eating freeze-dried or evaporated fare, we opt for foods such as macaroni and cheese, baked beans, and energy bars.

FLASHLIGHT

The trail at night can be a very dark place and finding one's way can be a challenge without some type of light. We prefer a headlamp for our trips into the woods; in the dark they're like a third hand. You can wear it or hold it as a regular flashlight. The ones we carry offer standard halogen lighting and a red night vision option. We recommend ones powered by double or triple-A batteries, because they're the easiest batteries to find and replace. In addition to a headlamp we also bring a small lantern that runs on double-A batteries; push it up and you have light, close it and you don't.

When packing light, this is our complete kitchen, with the exception of the spoons we carry.

Standard head lamp that runs on AA batteries.

CAMERAS

We're fine art photographers and although you're probably not, we want to take a moment to discuss camera gear. If you want to capture your trip with photographs and video, we'd like to suggest a couple different ideas. Most phones today have excellent cameras that can take stunning photographs and videos, and people seem to always want to have their phone with them, no matter what they're doing. You might consider buying a waterproof case for your digital phone that allows you to take pictures with your phone inside the protected case. We also suggest securing it with a lanyard. The lanyard will protect your phone from ending up at the bottom of a lake or swept away with the current. Your other option would be to buy a waterproof camera. You can find quality waterproof cameras in the $100 to $300 range. I prefer a Nikon CoolPix W300 and keep one in a pocket on my PFD. Other excellent choices are made by FugiFilm, Panasonic, and Olympus. If you do decide to bring your expensive digital camera, we recommend you buy a waterproof camera case that incorporates protective padding. This will not only keep the camera dry but also, protect it from all the bouncing and banging around that seems to wear on equipment when we use them in the great outdoors.

Our Camera Gear

Pictures help us reconnect with memories and no one knows that better than a photographer. As professional photographers heading into the field, we stuff as much photographic equipment as we can fit into our kit, without the additional weight sinking the canoe or kayak we're using, and then we stuff a little more in for good measure. We even bring equipment we don't expect to use. It's only along for the ride as insurance in the event our regular gear breaks down, gets lost, or ends up at the bottom of a lake. This is also why we carry a large amount of liability and equipment insurance.

Our regular kit for a canoeing trip includes two Canon SLR digital bodies; 5D Mk IIs, and four or five lenses; a 70-200 mm telephoto, 50mm normal, 24-70 mm telephoto, 16-35 mm wide angle, and a 24 mm macro lens. We also carry a mirrorless camera enclosed in an underwater housing, and two mirrorless cameras that we can pull out when we don't need to worry about them getting wet. I also keep a waterproof camera in one of the pockets on my PFD. We both bring our phones that second as cameras, and they're stored in waterproof cases either attached to our vests or to the deck of our boat. Our newest piece of photo gear is a drone with a Hasselblad camera, a great addition to our kit. There are places we just can't go to get the picture we want, and the drone sometimes makes that possible. Additionally, we pack; extra batteries, memory card wallets with extra cards, a tripod, camera raincoats, and cleaning equipment. Along with the camera gear we need to pack gear bags; a backpack to carry most of the camera gear when in the woods, and waterproof hard and soft cases for everything else. We also sometimes bring a laptop to download picture files; we aren't comfortable until we have two copies of our files in two different locations.

Checking on our 5D Mk IIs to make
sure they are still in working order
after a bumpy ride.

For all the equipment hassles and extra work it takes to capture the images we go after, we don't often complain about the added responsibility, especially after reading about the trials and tribulations of the photographer that accompanied Thomas Sedgwick Steele on his 1880 trip into the Maine Woods. The photographer was using the best equipment of his day and a development process known as wet plating, also known as the collodion process. In Steele's 1882 book, *Canoe and Camera, A 200 Mile Tour Through the Maine Forests*, he wrote about the effort required to produce an image for printing:

> Our artist was from the "Land of Steady Habits," whose sole duty it was to care for the delicate camera and glass plates, together with the necessary but ill-flavored bottles of his kit, and to be constantly on the alert for choice, or grand bits of scenery along the route. In such a tour as this with the many accidents ever attendant on camp life, it was no small matter to carry through the wilderness the articles pertaining to our photographer's kit.
>
> We had fifty glass plates six by eight inches each, which were prepared and developed on the ground by what is known as the "wet Process." Careless treatment in cartage on the "carries" or a sudden jar might at any moment damage them beyond recovery, which would immediately subvert one of the principal objectives of the exploration. Then each chemical had its individuality of importance, from the other to the collodion, the destroying of which would put an end to the pleasures of photographing.

This photographer must have had a real dedication to his art and the short narrative description by the author doesn't do justice to his constant struggle to keep things in order. He probably didn't have a lot of choices when it came to waterproof boxes and bags like we do today, nor was he able to take the photographs and wait to process them once he was out of the woods. He had to process his glass plates in a makeshift darkroom in the field and then transport the plates home without breaking them. He also needed to be vigilant with his chemicals; transported in glass bottles, if any of the containers broke during the trip, that was the end of the photography. I take my hat off to him and all those like him. The work he and others accomplished is remarkable, and they completed it under conditions I'll never have to deal with.

CLOTHING

Hat

We bring three hats on our trips; a baseball cap, wide-brimmed boonie hat or Stetson straw hat, and a watch cap. A baseball cap is standard head protection but is inadequate when out on a lake in the blazing summer sun making a straw hat perfect for sun protection. In the rain, nothing works better than a wide-brimmed boonie hat, a fan favorite of mine as a photographer, because of the crushable nature of the soft brim. We wear a watch cap when sleeping, and sometimes in the morning when there's a chill in the air. I pack mine inside my sleeping bag, so I know where it is when I need it.

Drying some of our gear after three days of rain.

The author with his full-coverage hat on pulling a kayak full of camera gear to a new shooting location.

My favorite 60/40 pants and, of course, I've already fallen into something.

Pants

You should bring two pairs of long pants and a pair of shorts or a bathing suit for a trip of three days or more. Some people love convertible pants because of the ease of changing from long pants to shorts. I'm not one of those people. Those pants tend to be too baggy for me and the zippers are never in the right place. The detached legs are also another item or items to keep track of, and as a photographer I'm keeping track of a large amount of gear to begin with and don't need loose leggings on my list. When I did wear this type of pants, I often lost at least one of the legs, which can be very problematic.

We usually bring one pair of quick drying, breathable pants. I prefer LL Bean's Riverton pants. They're 60/40 pants—60% cotton, 40% nylon, with seven pockets. I also bring a pair of lightweight, government-issue jungle fatigues. These are what I call my comfort pants. Old habits die hard, I guess.

For shorts, pack whatever is comfortable for you.

Shirts and Tops

Your shirts and tops should be light colored if possible, especially if your canoeing in black fly season. Black flies and mosquitoes are attracted to dark clothing, possibly because they absorb more heat than light colored clothing. We recommend a heavy shirt with pockets; either wool or fleece, a few t-shirts, a 60/40 long sleeve t-shirt— rash guard is the new buzz word, an insulated vest, and a wool sweater. I bring a hooded, cotton polyester, anorak type shirt that I love.

Base Layers

If you need long underwear, we recommend the new smart wool products. There are many other types on the market, but we'll stick with smart wool. It's expensive but worth every penny.

Footwear

You should have wet shoes and dry shoes. Wet shoes should be closed-toed, and traction soled. I'm one of those people who gets wet just being near water, requiring wet shoes that I can wear all day and in any kind of situation. I prefer the NRS Workboot Wetshoe. They're lace-up 5 mm neoprene, reinforced boots with good ankle support, and lugged bottoms. They function like wetsuit booties with a sole. You wear them without socks, and they keep your feet warm when wet or dry.

For dry shoes I pack my old standbys, Converse All-star low-cuts, and these days I bring two pairs. I sometimes wear them on the water, or when wading in moving water; they're much easier to slip out of if you get your foot stuck in a hole. I guess this makes all my shoes, wet shoes.

Rain Gear

You need a good set of rain gear for paddling any section of the trail because it's likely you will encounter inclement weather. A rain jacket and pants are your best choice. It's a personal preference whether you bring a rain jacket that fits under or over your PFD; mine fits under my life jacket. Pants should be loose enough to not constrict your paddling activity but no so large, as to entangle you in the water if you go overboard. Ponchos aren't recommended for paddling. If you go into the water wearing a poncho, there's a good chance, you'll become entangled in it and be unable to control your ability to get free. It's like trying to swim in a trash bag.

My 35-year-old fire gloves once belonged to my buddy Brad, and tag along for memory's sake, on all my trips.

Gloves

Gloves are a personal preference. Some people bring paddling gloves, some wear gloves in cold weather. I bring a pair but only use them for tending the fire. I pack a pair of uninsulated rawhide leather gloves in the same place as the saw or hatchet so I can find them when needed.

OTHER THOUGHTS ON GEAR

There are lots of other items people have on their packing lists that they believe they need to bring on canoeing trips and even though I try to pack as little as possible, I, like everyone else, have my list of things I'm more comfortable bringing than leaving home. I usually pack writing material. It's important for me to write about my experience and the writing is best done in concert with the experience. I also bring a small camping pillow. It aids sleep, and it fits into my sleeping bag stuff sack, so I view it as a minimal addition. Extra socks, underwear, and a baseball cap often get stuffed in my gear bag, and I will on occasion pack an extra raincoat. If there's any room left in my bag, I take a hooded sweatshirt. They don't pack well and become dysfunctional if they get wet, but they're great to sleep in.

ON THE TRAIL

The trail covers approximately 740 miles, and includes 22 streams and rivers, 58 lakes and ponds, and 53 miles of portaging divided among 63 "carries," and unless you plan on canoeing in a straight line from Old Forge to Fort Kent you're going to paddle more than 740 miles, and weather conditions, both wet and dry, will dictate how much canoe carrying is required. Many rivers and streams become unnavigable during dry conditions and require extra portaging. Wet conditions can also change the narrative; sometimes creating more portaging "opportunities," sometimes less, depending on what portion of the trail you're paddling. Eric and I encountered ice on some slower waters of the Androscoggin River and northern lakes in late spring, requiring us to either portage or turn around. We also encountered high water in places that sometimes was our friend; the Upper Ammonoosuc river was an easy paddle waterwise with spring runoff, and on the Upper Allagash section of the AWW, fall rain allowed for a much easier paddle than we'd anticipated although in some places it created challenging white water.

The best guidebooks and maps for this trail are the official maps and books sold by Mountaineers Books and Northern Forest Canoe Trail (northernforestcanoetrail .org). The trail is broken up into 13 contiguous maps that show all the information needed to successfully navigate the trail, however they are not topographic maps and we highly recommend you bring an official topo map of the area as well; they contain valuable information not contained on the NFCT maps.

1. Adirondack Country (West) New York
2. Adirondack North Country (Central) New York
3. Adirondack Country (East) New York
4. Islands and Farms Region Vermont
5. Upper Missisquoi Valley Vermont/Quebec
6. Northeast Kingdom Quebec/Vermont
7. Great North Woods New Hampshire
8. Rangeley Lakes Region Maine,
9. Flagstaff Region Maine
10. Greater Jackman Region Maine
11. Moosehead/Penobscot Region Maine
12. Allagash Region (South) Maine
13. Allagash Region (North) Maine

Since we're section paddlers, we also rely on the Delorme Atlas and Gazetteer's for the individual states to get us where we need to be. There's nothing like extensive planning for the wet part of the journey only to get lost on the road. We don't take these with us on the water, but they are an invaluable asset when we're traveling around the countryside. We also have GPS in our vehicles but as others can probably attest, it doesn't always function in Northeast backwoods areas.

Northern Forest Canoe Trail
An historic water trail through
New York, Vermont, Québec,
New Hampshire,
and Maine
GUESTBOOK
Northern Forest Canoe Trail
Sign-in Book
Old Forge, NY
Please Sign-in
The information you provide could be used to:
-Guide trail management
-Monitor and plan for degrees of trail use
-Aid emergency responders in search and rescues
Thank you for taking the time to sign-in!
As usual, feel free to call and let us know how your trip was: (802)496-2285
The NFCT is comprised of public and private land. Please respect all landowners and thank them when you can. Without their generousity your trip would not be possible.
You Are Here
www.northernforestcanoetrail.org

NFCT CAMPSITES

There are primitive, usually single campsites along the entire trail. Some are NFCT managed sites, while others are managed by the states. The sites along the Allagash are managed by the State of Maine and are equipped with a fireplace, table and outhouse. In New York, many of the primitive sites have lean-tos along with the standard fire ring and outhouse. Most sites are first-come, first served, but others require a reservation. There are also NFCT campsites on private land with their own sets of rules.

Primitive campsite along the trail.

Some sites require registration at a regional office, some require fire permits. The best decision regarding these primitive sites is to check the camping requirements for the section of the trail you're paddling.

CAMPGROUNDS

The best campgrounds in our experience are state run, and most states take great pride in the quality of their sites. Brown Tract Pond and Fish Creek in New York, Rangeley Lake State Park and Lilly Bay in Maine, are some of the parks we stayed in during our NFCT travels, and they all scored high marks with us. We were able to launch directly onto the trail from many of these campsites which was a great advantage for us, especially during our exploration of Moosehead Lake and the Saranacs. If you decide to stay at any of the state campgrounds in and around the trail, we highly recommend making reservations early in the process; the earlier the better if you want to choose the most advantageous spots.

Lean-to campsite in New York's Adirondacks.

Pelletier's Campground on the St. John River in St. Francis Maine; last stop before Fort Kent.

New York State Park

SPORTS CAMPS

The best sports camps are in Maine, and when we say sports we aren't talking about football and baseball. These camps are traditional hunting and fishing camps, once visited by "sports," the name given to city "slickers" who came to the North Woods in search of outdoor adventure. Sports were assisted by guides, another traditional institution associated with the state of Maine. Most sporting camps are located on a lake or river and have a central lodge for dining surrounded by cabins. Lakewood Camps on Lower Richardson is a historic camp we spent time visiting. Remote and out of the way, there are only a couple ways to get there; by boat from South Arm, float plane from Rangeley Lake, or if travelling on the NFCT, by portaging from Umbagog on the carry road.

Maynard's-In-Maine located in Rockwood on the Moose River is another historic sports camp, that we've spent time at. Unlike Lakewood Camps, Maynard's is very accessible. After arriving in Rockwood on Route 16, cross the bridge over the Moose River and take a left at the big sign, you can't miss it.

B&BS AND MOTELS

Motels, hotels, and B&Bs are plentiful anywhere the trail passes close to civilization. Obviously, you aren't going to find many in places like the Allagash but then you shouldn't expect to.

The Stark Village Inn located on the Upper Ammonoosuc River in Stark, NH.

IN AN EMERGENCY

We don't have a list for emergency sleeping arrangements because there aren't any. We do have a philosophy though: Camp anyplace you can if you're dealing with bad weather or safety concerns. Just do it quietly and unobtrusively. There aren't many people who will fault you if you're dealing with issues beyond your control and you set up in a place that you aren't "allowed" to pitch your tent. It's easier in a pinch to get forgiveness than it is to get permission, and safety is your trump card anytime you need to make an important decision for yourself or others.

CLEAN–DRAIN–DRY

Invasive species are non-native organisms that invade ecosystems, usually with devastating results. Intentionally or not, these species often destroy the natural stasis of a balanced environment and once introduced are almost impossible to remove. Today, anyone canoeing along the Northern Forest Canoe Trail will see signs explaining the Clean–Drain–Dry program. They will also more than likely be stopped by members of an inspection team checking for evidence of possible invasive species, as they attempt to halt their migration. Aquatic invasives like Asian watermilfoil, and curlyleaf pondweed—two destructive aquatics, have been found in many but not all, of the trail's waterways. Other plants known as terrestrial invasives include purple loosestrife—that pretty looking purple flowering plant often seen these days growing unchecked along streams and wetlands. As colorful as it is, it's choking off natural species like Cat-o'-nine-tails, an integral member of northeast wetland plant communities.

Responsible individuals, and hopefully that's most if not all of us, will inspect their canoe or kayak when they take their boat out of a waterway. In many places washing stations have been set up to clean boats which is the best way to prevent unintentional transport of non-native species from one water source to another. When portaging, and we do a lot of that on this trail, we should visually inspect and clean any foreign material from our canoes and kayaks before putting in again. When we portage, we try to bail out the water we may have taken into our canoe when we were on the water, before portaging to our new destination. We used to use a large sponge to help us with this task but have stopped that practice. A wet sponge can inadvertently transmit invasive species. They act like petri dishes unless properly dried, and even then, I find them suspect.

PORTAGING

Portaging is a large and varied component of the NFCT, and not the easiest way to enjoy the trail. The trail has an estimated 63 portages totaling 53 miles, but everything is relative, and in times of low water, many sections of the trail can't be paddled and require portaging.

The Nulhegan in Vermont, Upper Ammonoosuc in New Hampshire and the Dead River in Maine were all low water nightmares for us at different times during our NFCT adventure.

One of the many portage signs along the trail. This one is warning motorists that people are portaging along this section of roadway.

We jokingly refer to it as "land canoeing," a time when expectations and experience are literally turned upside down, and instead of sitting in a canoe and paddling, you're required to strap the canoe to your back and carry the boat and your belongings from one water source to another, often making three or four trips to move all the gear from water's edge to water's edge. If you're a through paddler, you'll need to portage all these miles, even more if water levels are down. As section paddlers we've figured out how to avoid many of these miles.

One portage we felt obliged to complete was the Mud Pond carry. Henry David Thoreau completed this section of the trail in 1857 and being Thoreau enthusiasts, we had the urge to try it. We were told this portage was a rite of passage and a memory we would hold for years to come, but when we found our experience was eerily like Thoreau's, we decided to do an about-face. We've both collected a pile of rites for a multitude of passages, making it easy, for us to decide, retracing Thoreau's land voyage, was a rite we didn't need to collect. Thoreau commented eloquently on his Mud Pond excursion in his seminal work, *The Maine Woods*, so we thought we'd let him fill everyone in on the particulars:

We set forward again. The walking rapidly grew worse, and the path more indistinct, and at length, after passing through a patch of calla palustris, still abundantly in bloom, we found ourselves in a more open and regular swamp, made less passable than ordinary by the unusual wetness of the season. We sank a foot deep in water and mud at every step, and sometimes up to our knees, and the trail was almost obliterated, being no more than that a musquash leaves in similar places, when he parts the floating sedge. In fact, it probably was a musquash trail in some places. We concluded that if Mud Pond was as muddy as the approach to it was wet, it certainly deserved its name. It would have been amusing to behold the dogged and deliberate pace at which we entered that swamp, without interchanging a word, as if determined to go through it, though it should come up to our necks. Having penetrated a considerable distance into this and found a tussuck on which we could deposit our loads, though there was no place to sit, my companion went back for the rest of his pack. I had thought to observe on this carry when we crossed the dividing line between the Penobscot and St. John, but as my feet had hardly been out of water the whole distance, and it was all level and stagnant, I began to despair of finding it.

Eric and I didn't despair, we just backed out to the dry ground of Grande Marche Road, strapped on our portage wheels, and moved along the gravel expressway until we found the Telos Road ranger station where we put in for Chamberlain Lake.

In contrast to the Mud Pond Carry, there's the Rangeley Carry. It begins on the Lake's northern shore at the town of Rangeley's Lakeside Park. There's a dock for an easy landing for you and your gear, and an NFCT kiosk if you'd like to sign in to record your journey. Once you've organized your equipment, you can move down Park Road, past the basketball and tennis courts, past the Chamber of Commerce and a few other buildings before arriving at Main Street. If you'd like to visit the Rangeley Region Sports Shop—fishing is their specialty, cross the street and head on in. When we visited, I bought a Gray Ghost Streamer to photograph for the book. It was designed by Carrie Stevens a self-taught fly tier, from nearby Upper Dam, famous for her streamer flies. Before you venture into the store, you'll need to decide where to leave the canoe while shopping and how long you can shop before you need to retrieve the rest of the gear you left down by the lake. You could leave the canoe in a parking space although that seems a little risky, or maybe on the small "grass" lawn of the Red Onion restaurant next door. If you choose to park your boat at the Red Onion, you should probably go in and patronize the place; we did. Ask them to hold a table for you outside so you can watch your canoe while eating; just let them know you'll be right back after you fetch the rest of your gear. When finished eating, stay on the Onion side of the street and follow Main Street down to Pond Street. When you turn the corner, you'll see a little town park and the Ecopelagicon Shop, were you can park your boat and gear for a moment to finish the best part of the portage. Walk back to Main Street cross the street and check out the Rangeley boat that hangs on the outside of the Rangeley Lakes Historical Society. Rangeley boats are similar to

DANGER !
FALLS AHEAD
KEEP RIGHT
FOR PORTAGE

The Dead River below Flagstaff.

Adirondack boats; used for work and pleasure, they were favored by the guides who assisted "sports" from the big city, on fishing trips. After you've checked out the boat, move down the street past a couple buildings and stand in front of the Doc Grant sign. If you do that, you'll be standing on the 45th parallel, halfway between the equator and the north pole; don't know why I get such a kick out of doing that, but I do. One last thing to do before you leave and it's probably the best part of the whole portage experience; cross the street again and get an ice cream at the Pine Tree Frosty, it's a little piece of heaven and just what you need, because you're headed for the Dallas Carry and the Dead River.

Before you push off into Haley Pond, you should check out the Ecopelagicon. You might find something interesting. It's filled with fishing gear, outdoor clothing, and books to name just a small part of what they stock. You can also buy or rent a kayak or canoe if someone stole yours while you were eating at the Onion.

Haley Pond is a quiet little pond, ideal for boating around in, but if your paddling the trail it's only a small respite before you shoulder your canoe again and begin another portage, and 3.5 miles of that carry is along the soft shoulder of Route 16; miserable, loose sandy soil not conducive to walking.

We knew the water was low on the South Branch of the Dead River, and that meant lots of additional miles; dragging, pulling and portaging, with multiple carries to move all our gear, along Route 16 with its whizzing cars and trucks. Our decision for this part of the trail was simple. We retrieved our truck, loaded it up, waved goodbye to Haley Pond, and portaged our way to Flagstaff Lake in two-wheel drive.

Flagstaff Lake is a manmade lake that sits on the former site of a small town named after Benedict Arnold's planting of a flagpole (flagstaff) on his march through the Maine wilderness to attack Quebec during the American Revolution. Looking south, the Bigelow mountain range can be seen in the distance.

Eric cooking another rainy-day lunch along the trail.

COOKING AND EATING

STOVES

There are many types of camping stoves big, small and in between, and fueled with a variety of flammable sources; propane, gasoline, butane, and wood. For many years on backpacking trips we carried a white gas stove, or a propane stove when camping in a campground. For canoeing trips, we use two different types of stoves; butane and wood. Both stoves are small, and their job is basically to boil water. The butane stove comes in two basic pieces; a base which is the fuel canister and the top piece; a burner head that screws on to the can. We also utilize a small plastic leg stabilizer because this type of stove configuration is top heavy.

If you go on a guided canoe trip, it's likely the food will be a big part of the trip. Guides usually cook over a campfire or on larger stoves, often using reflector ovens to make bread, muffins, and other outdoor delicacies. If you go with us, you'll be underwhelmed because all we do is boil water.

We bring three stoves; a stick stove and two Canister Stoves. Canister stoves are small, easily maintained, and once they're screwed on to a fuel can, they're ready to go. The two we carry are small enough to fit in your pocket and that's a plus when weight is a concern. We have an Etekcity Ultalight ($15.00) which comes in a small plastic container about the size of a box of paperclips, and an MSR Pocket Rocket 2 ($44.00). We also bring an MSR Universal Fuel Canister Stand ($15.00). It helps stabilize the

Stove head.

stove and can be used on any brand of fuel canister. Our wood stove is an Ohuhu Stainless Steel Backpacking Stove ($17.00). We use this if we run out of canister fuel, or sometimes just because it feels like a mini campfire, and we love campfires.

FOOD

Our food philosophy in the woods is simple; we rehydrate freeze dried or dehydrated food with hot water and call it dinner, and as true today as it was in 1880 when Thomas Steele and friends canoed the Maine Woods with their hard tack, salt pork, chow-chow and potted ham; after a hard days travel, almost any kind of camp food tastes superb.

> A "camp appetite" is something entirely different from what one enjoys at home. One would turn in aversion from the plainness of the fare where it placed on the table. But the surroundings and the daily vigorous exercise seem to make one forget the homely dishes, and articles refused at our own boards are devoured in the woods with avidity.   –Thomas Sedgwick Steele, 1880–*Canoe and Camera*

Eric and I break down food into three categories but unlike what you might think, it's not breakfast, lunch, and dinner; it's trail food, diners, and the like, and ice cream.

Trail food has morphed in recent years and I'm amazed at the choices on the market today. Many years ago, my buddy Brad and I, were getting ready for a backwoods breakfast and going through our usual routine. Our small white-gas stove with its missing heat shield, was whining and hissing as we sat and waited for the water to boil. There was a good chance the stove would over-pressurize and blow, so we positioned the release valve away from us, in the event it became a flamethrower.

The stove hissed, the water boiled, coffee was made, and for the first time we had scrambled eggs for breakfast in the mountains. What once looked like yellow cotton candy in a plastic bag was transformed into a thick yellow goo, and because we were sitting on a granite cliff 3,400 feet above sea level, attempting to summit Mt. Madison, with seven emotionally disturbed adolescents in tow; these were the best eggs we'd ever had. That was 1978, and the first time we'd tried this kind of food; the kind where you pour hot water in a bag, shake it over your head, wait two minutes, and eat. It was magic, and from that point forward, we couldn't get enough of that stuff for a couple reasons; it was easy to make, and it lightened our load, a great plus since weight was one of our biggest challenges.

I've had all sorts of hiking, camping, and climbing food; freeze dried, evaporated, smoked and salted since that magical moment over 40 years ago, and my camp appetite has almost always declared it, fantastic. The recipes have changed, the packaging has become more high tech, and in today's arena of food in a bag, instead of making scrambled eggs by shaking a bag of yellow goo over my head, I can pour hot water into a bag and serve up "best that I've ever had"; Mushroom Risotto, Thia Curry, or Chinese Pad Thai, at least that's how it tastes when I'm in the woods.

When not in the woods we're usually on the hunt for a diner or roadhouse, something unique, and eclectic, with history. We aren't looking for the best food we can find, but rather a place we can experience. If we're lucky, it's some place that time forgot, a place with stories pressed into its cracked floor tiles, creaky wooden booths, and worn china mugs, the kind of places new retro eateries try unsuccessfully to imitate, and we've found some great ones. We want to share these places with you, but since this isn't a book about our-of-the-way and out-of-date eateries, we'll share a few of the ones from the beginning of our journey and let you discover others along the trail for yourselves. Happy hunting.

THE BELVEDERE–SARANAC LAKE

The Belvedere is an old Roadhouse in Saranac Lake oozing with personality, and good food. I don't think they've changed the décor since 1940 but that just adds to the charm. The steps are cracked, the neon sign is a little tilted, but the food is great. It feels as though it's a little beyond its time, like an old man who's outlived all his friends, but still hanging on; a man comfortable in his own skin and unconcerned about what people may or may not think about him.

THE DRAKE'S INN–INLET

We drove past the Drake a few times before we stopped in. The peeling paint didn't bother us, neither did the checkered curtains nor the worn varnished booths. The Drake is a place that forgot to close. It's out of date, out of time, and out of place, and that's why it's such a jewel. When movies try to replicate an eatery from the 1940s or 50s, they should buy the blueprints for this place. I think I actually felt myself walk through a time warp when I entered; I had to keep looking out the window to see if we actually drove to the place in our new Ford truck, or was my old 1950 Oldsmobile Rocket 88 sitting in its place. The food was okay, but we weren't there to critique the

BELVEDERE
RESTAURANT

food, we were there to experience the aura. Yes, it sounds corny, but we don't care. We know something others don't; maybe that's why occasionally, one of us blurts out *"I wonder what they're serving at the Drake tonight?"*

CLAIR AND CARL'S–PLATTSBURG

We'd heard about the Michigan Hot Dog and since the word on the street was to go to Plattsburg, and we were going there anyway, that was our mission. The NFCT rolls into and through the city of Plattsburg with numerous rapids and dams creating

a number of portaging opportunities so we drove around this section on our way to Lake Champlain and the Vermont part of the trail, but before leaving we needed to hunt down lunch and a place that served these hot dog legends was on our radar. We have no idea what story to believe about how or why these hot dogs came to be, nor does it matter, we're just happy they're all legends.

We were lucky and hit gold finding Clare and Carl's; an unassuming, crooked, sinking into the ground building, that's been in business since 1942 and possibly the most famous of all the Michigan hotdog stands. And as legendary as legends are, someone also passed along the Clair and Carl's secret recipe, and here it is:

Hot dog
Hot dog bun
Yellow mustard
Michigan Sauce (see below)
Chopped onions

MICHIGAN SAUCE

4 tsps. chili powder
2 tsps. cumin
2 tsps. red pepper (crushed red pepper)
2 tsps. black pepper (I halved and was fine)
2 tsps. minced onion
1 tbsp. Hot Sauce.
24 oz. tomato sauce
2 lbs. lean ground beef

Put ingredients in a slow cooker, mash down with a potato masher to eliminate the chunks. Cook 6–8 hours in a slow cooker. Place the hot dog in a warm bun, place a line of yellow mustard across the dog. Spoon the Michigan Sauce over the hot dog and mustard; sprinkle with chopped onions over the Michigan Sauce. Then eat.

CRITTERS

CHIPMUNKS

Chipmunks are on the list because they can be found anyplace on the trail, especially around campsites. They're omnivores, they spend most of their time on the ground, and feed on different kinds of food including; nuts, seeds, berries, and sometimes grass. These little creatures weigh less than a pound, live an average of 2.5 years and spend most of that time looking for food. They are at home in a woodland  setting but can and will accustom themselves to almost any place if there's enough ground cover. They made our list because they often show up in and around campsites at state and local parks. They've figured out it's a good place to find food since humans are around and their crumbs and loosely packed snacks are a good source of food. We were able to photograph the chipmunks for this book because they got into some of the snack food we'd packed for our day on the river. If you look closely, you might even see some stolen Chex cereal close to the little critter's feet.

THE GREAT BLUE HERON

The Great Blue Heron is the largest heron in North America and can be seen all along the NFCT. A member of the heron/egret family it tends to live in and around; swamps, marshes, tidal flats, and coastal bays. Not usually together in groups, they are solitary hunters often seen standing or wading silently in shallow water, pensively staring at potential prey along the shoreline, or flying overhead in a slow glide with its head pulled back, and long skinny legs hanging behind its body like some prehistoric beast. When they're seen in groups it's usually a loose affiliation of birds clustered together because of an abundant food source. Accustomed to wading for food, they locate their prey by sight and pluck it out of the water using their long beak. They rarely venture far from water and can often be found in populated areas if there's a good food supply. These solitary hunters usually nest in trees to avoid predators, and only come together during the breeding season.

BEARS

Black bears are the largest population of bears in the United States and are found all along the trail. We spotted one in our travels, and all we got to see was its hind end as it ran away. Winnie the Pooh, Smokey the Bear, and Teddy Bear are all manifestations of the Black bear, and although well-meaning people find pleasure in anthropomorphizing creatures like bears, they are undomesticated wild animals. The good news is most black bears are shy and would rather run away from humans than have to deal with them.

A black bear's biggest activity is eating, and to stay healthy an average bear needs to eat between 11 to 18 pounds a day; that's a lot of berries, and one of the reasons, bears are solitary animals, they need a fair amount of acreage to shop. Their diet is mostly vegetarian and includes; nuts, berries, fruits, roots and grasses, but they aren't picky, nor can they be. They also eat, bees, ants, and grubs when they find them, and carrion. If you run into a bear in the woods or on the trail, back away slowly and remove yourself from the situation. Running away or climbing a tree to get away from

We did see one bear who ran away before I could photograph him, but I had more luck with this kind.

a bear is not an effective practice. Bears can run very fast and black bears are adept at climbing trees.

If one enters your camp, your party should group together and act as a unit. You can also stretch your arms out to make yourselves look even bigger. Black bears are not aggressive by nature and grouping together gives the bear the impression of something larger than himself and he'll usually leave you along. If you practice good campground etiquette and keep your food secured, a bear probably doesn't have any reason to start going through your belongings.

BUGS AND SUCH

There are some pesky little creatures along the trail that seem to want to bother us to no end at times, persistent little buggers with the potential to drive us to temporary insanity or at least give us that impression. We'll discuss them shortly, but interestingly we seem to have some of them listed upside down in terms of health risks, or at least I have. I've always had leeches at the top of my list followed by ticks, then mosquitoes, however leeches pose a minimal health risk while the other two transmit disease; lime disease in the Northeast by ticks, and encephalitis, the Zika and West Nile virus, by mosquitoes. In the northeast we often consider mosquitoes more of a nuisance than anything else even though they kill more people worldwide than any other creature on earth and have the potential under the right conditions to wipe out the human race.

BLACK FLIES

Someone once asked me if when they went to the woods, would they be able to tell if the bugs flying around them were black flies. I responded; "No worries. If they're black flies, they'll introduce themselves." You can always tell when someone's been involved with black flies; their neck, arms and face are covered in welts and scabs from fly bites. Black flies are true flies and are active most of the spring and summer in the northern forest, with the biggest activity occurring during what's known as Black Fly Season, from mid-May to mid-June when they are at their peak. They can be brutal, persistent, seemingly omnipresent little buggers, that you don't hear coming; silent, little creatures until they decide to take a chunk out of you; a bite that can sometimes leave a swollen wound as big as a golf ball. Even the ones that don't bite, and there are a few black fly species that don't, will attempt to get in your ears, nose and mouth.

Black flies are attracted to dark colors, possibly because those colors absorb more heat but don't think all you need to do is wear a white t-shirt in the woods during black fly season, they're out to get everyone especially those of us who are warm blooded. They go after livestock and moose as eagerly as they go after humans and have been known to drive moose straight out of the woods in search of relief.

MOSQUITOS

Who hasn't had the experience of a mosquito buzzing around his or her head, close enough to hear them as they search in the dark of night for a good place to sting you? You swing and swat at the sound only to realize you missed, and she's coming in for another bombing run. Just the idea of that keeps me up at night once I realize "they're in my tent."

I hate mosquitoes. I understand they probably serve some purpose in the food chain and some ecological balance with other species, but I don't care; I have no use for them. Beyond the buzzing around my head and the biting or I guess I should say stinging, they're also great carriers and spreaders of disease, some deadly; West Nile virus, Equine Encephalitis, and the Zika virus, to name a few that are relevant to the northeast. The West Nile virus attacks a person's neurologic system, while Equine Encephalitis causes an infection in the brain, both can be life threatening for those at risk.

NO-SEE-UMS

It doesn't really matter if you don't know what a no-see-um looks like or what kind of no-see-um you're up against: sand flee, sand fly, flying midge, or punky. It's enough to know they breed near streams, wetlands, beaches and riverbeds, and if some little bug, correction, a herd of little bugs, smaller than a black fly are silently attacking you and drawing blood as they bite chunks out of your hide, they're probably no-see-ums and you need to exit the area. I've read that these small flesh eaters don't travel far from home and it helps to move away from these silent little carnivore's hatch-site but sometimes there are hundreds of little groups with hundreds of little homes and your only relief is probably to bathe yourself in bug repellent or retreat to your tent. These little creatures are also small enough to pass through some screens making mesh size an important requirement to consider when buying a tent. Look for tents with screens fine enough to keep these little buggers out or prepare to do battle with these persistent little pests. It's only the females that do the biting, but these little creatures also fly into a person's; eyes, ears, mouth and nose; not a pleasant experience.

TICKS

Ticks are external parasites that live off the blood of humans and other warm-blooded animals. There are two ticks to be concerned about in the northeast along the NFCT and both can spread disease; the dog tick, sometimes referred to as a wood tick, is known to spread Rocky Mountain Spotted Fever and the deer tick also known as the blacklegged tick is the transmitter of Lyme Disease. The dog tick is the larger of the two and ranges in size from ⅛ of an inch before feeding to ½ inch long after. Deer ticks are about half the size of a dog tick making them hard to spot sometimes. They range from 4 mm long before feeding to 10 mm after a blood meal.

There are a lot of ideas floating around about how to remove a tick. Some will tell you to coat the tick with petroleum jelly to smother it, others will suggest burning it off with a match, or coating it in some other goo, but none of these techniques are effective or recommended and some can actually compound the problem. The easiest way to remove a tick is to pull it off with a set of pointed tweezers or by using some of the specialized tick removing tools that have recently come on the market. Our tick remover is a small plastic tool known as a Ticked Off. It's a little plastic spoon with a V cut out of it. You simply scoop the tick with the notch and pull him off. You should clean a tick wound with rubbing alcohol or soap and water. If the head does break off while you're attempting to extract it, do the best you can to remove the head and them clean the wound.

LEECHES

There are leeches on the trail most notably on the Missisquoi River, and although leeches don't transmit disease to humans and extract less blood than your average hospital test before detaching themselves, many people are genuinely freaked out by them and agree with Humphrey Bogart's character Charlie Allnut in the African Queen when he says; "If there's anything in the world I hate it's leeches—filthy little devils!"

Leeches aren't filthy, and don't transmit disease like the other buggers we've discussed and are basically harmless, so what's the big deal? Maybe it's the idea that there's an army of ugly blackish brown worm-like creatures below the waterline hunting us down to suck our blood. Ugh, I'm a little freaked out just writing this stuff!

If you do find a leech on your body the best way to remove it, is by grasping it and pulling it off. Don't try to burn it or cut it off, don't jerk it left or right, and don't try to slap it or brush it away. Simply pull it straight off as gently as possible. The wound may bleed more than usual because of the blood thinning chemical that remains in the wound but there's no health issue. Simply treat the wound as you would any other cut and you should be fine. I still agree with Charlie though: If there's anything in the world I hate, it's leeches, even if they aren't filthy little devils.

Dragonfly nymphs look ominous but they don't attack humans and should be protected since they eat the bugs that like to bite us, by plucking them right out of the sky. Nymphs are the middle stage in a three-stage process (egg, nymph, adult) known as incomplete metamorphosis. You can see a picture of an adult dragonfly on page 172.

NEW YORK: 147 MILES

The New York section of the trail is 147 miles long, beginning in the hamlet of Old Forge at First Lake of the Fulton Chain of Lakes, and ends at Plattsburg New York on the western shore of Lake Champlain. The trail includes Raquette Lake and River, Long Lake, and the Saranac Chain of Lakes. It includes one of the most unique sections of the trail known as Brown's Tract Inlet, home to; fish, beaver, bear, deer, and carnivorous pitcher plants. Maps 1–3 cover this section of the trail.

We love being on the water but spent the better part of our first day in transit to the Adirondacks discussing what opportunities we might have to photograph wildlife. We would shoot early in the morning and late into the afternoon when some animals tend to be more active but beyond that, we would simply try to be ready for the moment when subjects presented themselves; easier said than done, but that was the plan. We arrived at Brown Tract Pond Campground in Raquette Lake—our base for the next five days of canoeing late in the afternoon, and even before saying hello to the ranger, we were greeted with; "We have bears, so please pay attention to the following rules!" The ranger then went on to explain the food rules. "Don't store food in your tent. Don't even bring food into your tent! Don't store food in the back of the truck, your vinyl cover isn't going to stop a bear from getting in, it's just going to make is a bigger mess when they do." "Store all—and she meant all our food, in closed containers inside the cab of our truck with the windows rolled, up and dispose of any

leftovers at the recycling center." This bear alert was further reinforced by our view of the recycling center with its heavy gauge electrified fence and warning signs. The bears she was talking about were American black bears, indigenous to the northeast United States and most of Canada, and she was making it clear that they weren't the problem, people were.

The campground became our base for day trips. We were unfamiliar with the Adirondacks and much like the early American settlers; we'd spent a lot of time both east and west of the Adirondacks but not in the Adirondacks, so this would be our first big adventure in the largest state park east of the Mississippi River

We registered, set up camp secured our food and headed to Old Forge to check things out and plan our activities for the following day. Old Forge is part of the town of Webb in Herkimer County, New York whose primary business is tourism. Restaurants, eclectic retail stores and gift shops fill the downtown, with the largest attraction located just across the street from the launch point for the NFCT on Route 28; it's the Enchanted Forest Water Safari, New York's largest water theme park. The park overflows with exotically named water rides including; the Amazon, Kilimanjaro, and the Nairobi Narrows, and families drive from miles around each summer to experience its make-believe adventures. The more I stared at the theme park's packed parking lot, the more I wondered why these people were spending all sorts of money to go on water rides in a make-believe theme park. Why didn't they just cross the street and experience the real thing.

The trail begins in the heart of Adirondack Park, but it skirts the high wilderness of the park's interior, opting instead to follow the swollen Moose River, known today as Fulton Chain of Lakes. The dam that helped create the Chain was built in the

OLD FORGE

early days of settlement and sits today, next to the NFCT kiosk on Old Forge Pond. Launching at the pond can feel daunting but not because you're about to embark on a wilderness adventure. No, it's daunting because of the amount of boat traffic. The pond is surrounded by commercial property including; hotels, motels, and marinas, creating at times a traffic jam of watercraft, all trying to maneuver the channel along with the mail and tour boats that call this little pond their home. After paddling through the channel that connects the pond to the Chain, we entered First Lake, another active area dotted with shoreline camps and cabins, many with boathouses. The traditional Adirondack boat house is a two-story affair that sits over the water with doors on the lower section allowing the owner to drive his boat into its "garage." The upper floor is for storage or relaxation; a place to sit and watch the world go by, or at least the boaters if that's what you like to do.

First, Second and Third Lake all feel like one lake, at least from the vantage point of a canoe. They're connected to one another by short narrows and we had no problem navigating them. I wasn't sure the passenger boats would fit at least through one of the sets, but they seem to have no problem at all. The connection to Fourth Lake is through an even narrower channel, still not a problem for our shallow draft canoe but somewhat challenging for the larger tour boats that travel up and down the lakes.

Fourth Lake is a big lake and the largest lake in the chain, and although we had some trouble with the wind, our destination was the village of Inlet at its northern end, and we were determined to get there. Wind is the danger when traveling on any of these lakes but especially on Fourth Lake. It can pick up and roll south or west any-time weather conditions dictate and when it blows, it blows hard. When this happens, the lake becomes a frothing sea of whitecaps and is best paddled close to shore along the Route 28 side. Our Old Town Voyager has no keel and is sensitive to wind which can make paddling on a lake with rough "seas" challenging, especially if we're carrying a light load. The wind cooperated for us on day 1 and the whitecaps didn't develop until our second day when we launched from Inlet on our way to Fifth Lake. Our saving grace, that day was the short amount of paddling we needed to do to get to the channel. After launching at the boat ramp down the street from Arrowhead Park we only had to paddle out past the swimming markers, around to the left past the break-water, and into the channel that would bring us to Fifth Lake.

Inlet is 11 miles from Old Forge and a good place to stop after your first day of paddling, especially if the wind was blowing you around and you were being pounded by white caps. If you paddled to Inlet in inclement weather, you may have paddled quite a few extra miles because of the wind. The village is what we'd consider a trail town. It has everything you need if you forgot something or lost some of your gear. We hadn't lost anything at this point, so we pulled our boat out of the water at the landing and headed up the street to a pizza shop for lunch. The restaurant's back door looks out onto the channel. After lunch we headed over to Kalil's Grocery Store for a walk-around, then over to the bookstore near Arrowhead Park for some local reading material, and finally to the Northern Lights Ice Cream Stand. We have a standing rule about ice cream, and it's a simple one; "Whenever and wherever."

Ice cream, one of the trails staples.

The channel between Fourth and Fifth Lake is a hubbub of activity. It harbors a marina, summer camps and cottages, and since it navigates so close to the village, it offers access to downtown, if you missed the landing next to Arrowhead Park, you can simply secure your vessel and walk up for lunch or shopping.

Fifth Lake is a small lake, a pond really, or maybe even a mud puddle of a water body. It sits in a small depression and is a quiet, calm place to paddle, until the cars and the down-shifting trucks break the silence. The pond sits tight against the roadway and the sound of traffic often interrupts the tranquility. A short paddle across the pond will bring you to the first carry of the trail. The carrying place also has an outhouse which can be a welcome site for many. The carry is short at first as you bring your gear up to the street. Crossing the street, you'll have a longer walk, although it's under a mile, to the put in on Sixth Lake. Sixth Lake is the second smallest lake in

At 6 million acres, 2.6 million public acres, and 3.4 million private, Adirondack Park in New York is almost as the size of the state of Vermont. It's the largest park in the lower forty-eight and one of only two areas in the world protected by constitution. In addition to the diverse population of animals and plants, the park is also home to 105 towns and 140,000 residents. Mechanized vehicles are prohibited from access to roughly 100-million acres of the park and are considered true wilderness.

the chain and filled with camps and cottages. It was flat calm and sunny the day we visited. Paddling under Seventh Lake Road we changed our plans when we arrived at Seventh Lake. We thought it was a good time to get a different perspective of the trail and elevation was what we needed, so we headed over to Payne's Air Service on Seventh Lake. Jim Payne and his son Tom have been flying people around the Adirondacks for years, often flying people in and out of the back country on wilderness fishing and camping trips. When we told them what we were doing, they were more than happy to take us up for a ride and show us around. I was impressed and knew we had the right flying team when I saw Tom methodically cleaning off the airplane's windows and pumping out the pontoons. And even more impressed with the amount of time they spent flying us around, pointing out parts of the NFCT, and then flying us around again so we'd have a better angle for shooting pictures, especially when the sun popped out. When all was said and done, they charged us the normal 15-minute sightseeing flight. We really appreciate those guys.

As we left the flight shack, I couldn't help but notice the sign hanging above the doorway, it read: *This isn't a park, this is our home were we work and live.* I asked about the sign but the only answer I got was; "Lot of rules around here."

Eighth Lake State campground is located at the southern end of the lake and if you want to explore this lake, I suggest you launch your boat at the campground's landing. You'll pay a day use fee for parking but it's worth it unless you're through paddling the Chain because trail access on the southern end is by portage, and the exit at the northern end is a portage as well.

Day three for us was going to be an exciting adventure down a unique section of the Northern Forest Canoe Trail; Brown's Tract.

From the air the day before, Brown's Tract looked like a slow-moving serpentine river plying its way from Eighth Lake through quiet swampy wetlands before emptying into Raquette Lake. No roads, traffic, or noisy boaters occupied this part of the trail. This section was naturally reserved for wilder creatures and we were excited at the possibility of exploring this place. A boardwalk had been built in 2008 and our plan was to access the river via this walkway and paddle out to the village of Raquette Lake, a short distance from the campground we were staying in. We'd only seen this structure from the air and weren't sure how to find it, so we asked for directions from a ranger.

"Go this way, then that way and then that way, again. Then look for a place on the right-hand side with a parking spot and a sign-in box and you'll be at the beginning of the trail to the boardwalk."

We thanked her for the directions and headed on our way, eventually finding the spot she was talking about. Packing our gear up we excitedly headed down the trail, through a boreal forest of large pines and scrub hardwoods, eventually coming to the beginning of what we thought was the boardwalk, but something wasn't right. From the pictures I'd seen the boardwalk was constructed out of wood and the one we were standing on was made of interlaced plastic pontoons but hey, how many boardwalks could there be leading into Brown's Tract. We quickly found out the answer to the

Brown Tract carnivorous pitcher plants.

question when we hiked to the end of the boardwalk, and the answer is two. There are two boardwalks that lead people into this swampy, buggy, wetland with a river. The one we were looking for that would bring us to the put-in, and the one we were standing on that simply ended in the middle of a bog with no way to get to the water. After a few choice words we hauled back and headed out of the woods to regroup but not before we realized our good fortune. We'd ended up in a bog filled with carnivorous pitcher plants; more pitcher plants than I'd ever seen together in my life. It was a Wizard of Oz moment; a moment where we ended up in the wrong place at the right time and got to witness something special. Then it was back to reality, and we packed up again and hauled our gear back to the truck.

We regrouped and decided to explore Brown's Tract from the Raquette Lake end in the afternoon, and after putting in at the boat-launch we headed to the riverway, but first we had to get over a beaver dam built across the creek. The technique for doing this is simple. Paddle hard into the dam and beach the canoe, at which point the bowman gets out and stands on the dam, steadying the boat while the stern man climbs forward and gets out on the other side of the canoe. Both paddlers then push and pull the canoe over the dam and repeat the process of unloading in reverse to get back into the boat. The dam was surprisingly sturdy, and the hauling went off without a hitch. The only drawback for me was the foul smell of rotting vegetation my sneakers gave off, for the remainder of the trip.

It wasn't a hard paddle for us, thank you very much, and just a few turns away from the bridge we found ourselves immersed in a narrowing trail of backwater wetland; a secluded safety zone for ducks who ignored our presence, and beaver who did not. There were numerous beaver lodges, those mud and stick mounds built by "eager" beavers as protection from the elements, their enemies, and of course us. I was in a fog staring at our immense green surroundings, when one of these busy creatures gave a warning shot across our bow, startling me out of my daydream. Their typical action when threatened—at least when I've encountered them, is to head directly towards you and let off a hard slap of their flat tail not unlike the crack of a gun, on the water's surface before diving for safety. I never saw him coming but couldn't miss hearing the tail slap.

Brown's Tract has a familiar smell. The mineral rich, boreal, backwater wetland, with its slow-moving water, is home to a variety of herbaceous plants including; water lily, pickerel weed, cattails and flag. And its smell is a byproduct of highly oxygenated, slow moving water that aids in the growth but also in the composting of plant life; a wet stagnant composting smell evident to anyone who stirs up its nutrient rich sludge.

It's also a protective environment for animals such as deer, beaver, ducks and raccoons. It's a safety zone inaccessible to many of its resident's enemies; a good place to live, or hide, and as the beaver and ducks seem to understand; to raise a family.

Beaver dam at the eastern entrance to Brown's Tract from Raquette Lake.

Brown's Tract Beaver Lodge.

Brown's Tract.

We spent a few hours snaking our way up and down the watercourse; cameras out in the hope of photographing a beaver or two but without luck. They were all probably still hiding after the hubbub of our first encounter. On our way back to Raquette Lake I thought I noticed some of the land move, and it was moving. The tract seemed to have a good amount of what some call floating islands or floating land. A boggy, peaty, landmass, made mostly of rotting plant material and held together by living plants, was sitting on the surface of the swamp without being attached to the bottom; basically floating around like a raft, a good place for fish to congregate, shielded from marauding predators and inaccessible to others; no Great Blue Heron poking around looking for dinner in this part of the wetlands.

As the sun began to set, we backtracked eventually returning to the bridge, which we slid under, and the beaver dam we climbed over as we reentered the lake where I washed out my sneakers and the inside of our canoe before we headed back to the campground to see if any bears had invited themselves for dinner.

Early morning paddle on Raquette Lake.<

Brown's Tract empties into Raquette Lake, and Raquette and Long Lake dominate this part of the trail. Both are big lakes and susceptible to high winds, especially Long Lake. We had our hands full with other trail work, not to mention the wind so we'll be back another time to do battle with this part of the trail. Beyond Long Lake lies more of the Raquette River. This section is punctuated with falls and rapids interspersed with divergent channels which can be disorienting and confusing. Don't miss the entrance to Stony Creek. The creek and pond will bring you to the Indian Carry. The one mile wheelable carry is your entranceway to the Saranac Lakes, and a successful traverse will bring you to the lower end of Upper Saranac Lake.

Raquette Lake General Store, home of the best doughnuts on the NFCT.

THE SARANAC LAKES

Rain hammered against our tent's nylon cover—a rain fly sitting inches above the tent's screened roof, protecting us in theory from inclement weather. It was day three of our second sojourn to upstate New York and day five of us living with this liquid sunshine, which meant we packed in the rain, drove in the rain, set up in the rain, and were now kayaking and exploring in the rain. The sun did poke its head out occasionally as a tease, but most of this trip was wet and rainy.

When you're damp and wet and all your gear is damp and wet, you become absorbed into the natural watery world around you and become one with the wetness; you feel as green as the soaked foliage around you and as fluid as the water you glide over.

Wind however, is a different story. I'm not a fan of the wind, a breeze yes, possibly a sailing wind if I'm rigged for it, but wind is the great antagonist for me, in and out of the water when I'm canoeing or kayaking, and today was one of those days.

Rain, wind, and now disorganized currents were competing to push us off our course. You can fight the wind, or you can fight the current but fighting both at the same time is an agonizing paddle, and that's the mess we found ourselves in. There have been times on this trip when the wind has blown so hard and erratic it drove us in one direction, while it pushed us in another, banging us around as we bobbed like a cork on a stormy sea with all the paddling control of a blind man with a stick, and today was one of those days. There were times we simply held our position no

matter how hard we fought, and for once, we needed to get some place by a certain time. We had an appointment on Eagle Island in Upper Saranac Lake to meet the caretaker of one of the last remaining Great Camps in this part of the Adirondacks. It was built in 1899 by William Coulter as a summer retreat for Levi Morton, onetime vice-president of the United States and Governor of New York. Camp Eagle Island is on the National Register of Historic Places and a National Historic Landmark and we were excited at the thought of visiting the property because even though it was a girl scout camp since 1938, and currently a new girl's camp today, most of the scouting activity that took place over the past 80-plus years was conducted outside many of the buildings, leaving much of the property in a weird state of suspended animation. We couldn't wait to see what we might find but we weren't really making any progress, and our headway problem was getting worse. We were now exposed to the winds blowing north from both Gull and Pelsky Bay with a weird crosswind from Gilpin Bay trying hard to spin us sideways to the danger. I could hear the wind gods whispering; "Welcome to the world of kayaking Mr. Tobyne and Mr. Alexander. Good

luck, and glad to have you aboard, or maybe, glad to have you overboard." This was the first time we'd kayaked on the trail, and the first time I'd even been in a kayak since I was 16. Lucky for us our choice of boats had been sound, and our little 10-foot flat bottom vessels were surprisingly sturdy against the heavy crosswinds; the boat's chined hulls allowing us to track straight into the angry whitecaps, which seemed like a good decision considering our limited experience. There was nothing pretty about this trip but if we held marginal control through maximum effort, we wouldn't founder or roll over. At least that was my hypothesis. Moving left allowed us to take less wind from Pelky Bay and pay more attention to the blow coming straight out of the south which reduced the chop significantly, and once we paddled beyond the northern tip of Eagle Island allowing us to slide under its lee, we entered calmer waters that became windless and glassine when we reached the cove that held the island's boathouse.

GREAT CAMPS

We were very excited to be visiting Eagle Island. We'd been told this Great Camp was "suspended in time," and if that was true, we were going to have the opportunity to visit a place that hadn't really changed since the industrialist Henry Graves Jr. owned it. The camp had been sold to a Girl Scout organization in 1938 and they'd opted to spend most of their time in tents leaving the buildings unchanged. Great Camps were built for the rich as another way to get away from the heat and pollution of the summer city. For those without means, summer months in most metropolitan areas were hot and smelly with bad air and excessive pollution, and for those with means and the ability to leave, anyplace was better than the big city in the summer, making the back-country—especially the Adirondacks, a valuable and entitled escape. The mid 1800s saw many of the rich from New York, Newark, Boston and other large metropolitan areas, migrating to the Adirondacks to live in camps for the summer although the definition of camp was a relative term. Much of this new relationship with nature for those who could afford it was spurred on by William H.H. Murray's publication, *Adventures in the Adirondacks*, a romanticized view of life in the woods. More propaganda than fact, it helped heighten interest in New York's wilder environs.

Healthfulness of Camp Life

I am often asked if ladies would not "catch cold" in the woods, and if the physical exertion which one must put forth is not such as to forbid that any, but robust people should undertake the trip. To this I reply that I believe it to be a physical impossibility for one, however fragile or delicate, to "catch cold" in this wilderness. Remember that you are here in a mountainous region where dampness and miasma, such as prevail in lower sections, are entirely unknown. Consider, too, how genial and equable is the climate in the summer months, and how pure and rarefied the atmosphere. Remember, also, that you breathe an air odorous with the smell of pine and cedar and balsam, and absolutely free from the least taint of impurity; and when you take all this into account, you will see how very dissimilar are the conditions and surroundings of life in the woods to life in the city or village. Acquainted as I am with many ladies, some of them accustomed to every luxury, and of delicate health, who have "camped out" in this wilderness, I have yet to meet with a single one who ever "caught cold," or experienced any other inconvenience to the bodily health in the woods. As to the "physical exertion," there is no such exertion known here. It is the laziest of all imaginable places, if you incline to indolence. Tramping is unknown in this region. Wherever you wish to go your guide paddles you. Your hunting, fishing, sight-seeing, are all done from the boat. Going in or coming out you cross the necessary carries, which, for the most part, are short and good walking, and you can take your own time for it. In this I refer, of course, to the most frequented parts of the wilderness, and not to the portions seldom visited and more difficult of access. There are sections which I have visited by dragging my cedar shell behind me up narrow creeks and through tamarack swamps, middle deep in mud

Landing at the dock on Eagle Island.

and water; but no guide would think of taking a party, unless urged by the party itself, into any such region; and, ordinarily speaking, there is no need of exertion which a child of five summers could not safely put forth, from one end to the other of a trip.

Great Camps were part of the Gilded Age, a place the rich could retreat to in summer, to get "back to nature" although they were in truth more like the rustic versions of Newport mansions. The "campers" participated in boat races, tennis tournaments and dinner parties, and the camps had all the furnishings of an affluent lifestyle. There was even a direct line installed from Wall Street to the Adirondacks allowing campers to keep an eye on their wealth. It was the stock market crash of 1929 in fact, that brought down the era of the Great Camps, as the rich either walked away from, gifted, or sold their properties.

As I mentioned, Eagle Island Great Camp was built in 1899 by William Coulter as a summer retreat for Levi Morton, onetime Vice-President of the United States and Governor of New York. Camp Eagle Island is on the National Register of Historic Places and a National Historic Landmark confirming its importance as an example of a traditional Adirondack retreat. In 1910 the camp was sold to industrialist Henry Graves Jr. who eventually donated it to the New Jersey Girl Scouts of the Oranges and Maplewood, in memory of his sons who'd died in car accidents, and it functioned as a

girls camp until it was sold to The Friends of Eagle Island whose vision is to preserve a place that "children may always play." The camp is set to reopen in 2020.

We landed at the boat house—half sinking and needing work, and could hear the sounds of construction from up above, so we headed toward the noise. It was a muddy mess because of the recent rains but work was going on in and around many of the buildings. So much work that we had to do a lot of tight photography. Broad wide-angle photography capturing mud, backhoes, staging and the numerous outhouses sprinkled around the property was not the plan, so we shot tight and used much of the surrounding property to mask the work areas. Our part of the bargain for getting on the island in the first place was a set of photographs the owners could use in their publications and we wanted to do the best job possible.

The views were extraordinary, both inside the buildings and out, and much of what we were able to document was once in a lifetime stuff. Eric at one point asked me if I thought any of the stuffed animal heads lining some walls, were from Girl Scout safaris. I suggested the answer was probably, not. Examples of Adirondack stick construction was everywhere as well as wonderful examples of the traditional use of covered porch camp construction that was used to connect multiple buildings.

Once we completed our photo shoot, it was back into the boats for another lesson. This time we were going to learn about the dangers of what sailors call, a following sea. A following sea can be dangerous and happens when your boat is moving in the same

direction as the waves, and if you encounter waves moving faster than you and your boat, they can overturn you from behind. Following seas or in this case lake current can push your boat forward and sideways taking control away from you the operator, and potentially capsizing the boat from behind. To stop this from happening and maintain control of your vessel you should match or better the speed of the waves. The trick is to paddle a little faster than the waves to maintain control of your vessel. Too fast and you could nose into the wave in front of you, to slow and the wave behind you can pick you up and push you forward or sideways wresting control away from you. At that point you can no longer steer the boat.

From Eagle Island to Fish Creek, our destination, we slipped and slid our way through the rolling waves, sometimes in control other times not, until we finally arrive in smoother waters. We paddled the last 30 minutes in a light drizzle and returned to

The Adirondack Mountains seen from Oseetah Lake.

Lower locks of Saranac Lake.

camp exhausted, so we opted to do a different kind of exploring. We went in search of a special place to eat, and we found it at a historic roadhouse; the Belvedere.

The following day brought a dry and clearing sky and breakfast was a pleasant experience for the first time in a while. For once I was drier than the coffee in my cup. We were headed to the Lower Saranac to explore Lower Saranac Lake, First and Second Ponds, Oseetah Lake Kiwassa Lake, and Lake Flower. We went through the obligatory invasive species inspection and with a clean bill we launched our kayaks at the State Bridge Boat Launch in search of anything and everything interesting and it didn't talk long. We found a huge beaver lodge on the side of Second Pond, large and impressive and a scattering of erratics scattered around the edges of the pond. On the eastern end,

we found the channel to Osseetah Lake; a narrow twisting channel littered with large boulders, downed trees and in places, a sea of stumps. The channel was marked by red and green buoys like the harbor back home and no wake signs scattered around. This is when we really fell in love with our little boats. We don't draft more than 2-inches even with a boatload of gear, and these little kayaks can fit into all sorts of small crannies. Just what we wanted for exploring. We visited our first New York trail campsite that included a leen-to; nice site but once off the water the woods were festering with insects; mosquitoes mostly. Around every corner we found a different scene; in one place another boulder field or scattered erratics; around the next bend, a field of dead trees and a stump cemetery; deep water one minute, a couple inches the next. We

This boulder is part of a seemingly out-of-place collection of large boulders, located in the middle of the channel between Second Pond on Lower Saranac Lake and Lake Oseetah. The Adirondacks like other sections of the trail are home to an assortment of giant boulders, some located in precarious places, others simply lying or scattered around the landscape. These large pieces of geological debris are leftovers from the last ice age when the Laurentide ice sheet, as the last great glacier to cover the Northeast, carved out the current landscape of New England and eastern Canada, as it retreated northward.

even took a ride at the Saranac's Lower Locks and dam. We needed to get to a lower elevation to enter Oseetah Lake and going over the waterfall didn't seem like the way to go. The locks were operated by an operator who chatted with us for a while, he wanted his picture taken to get in the book. Sorry Mike, or whatever your name was, that one didn't make the cut. The amazing thing about the locks are the written directions posted on a billboard you can't miss. If there's no operator present when you show up, you operate the equipment yourself; leaving your boat to run the show from the control booth. Amazing was my second thought, my first thought was; how much liability insurance does the State of New York have on this operation, to cover any issues that might pop up when they let an amateur run the show.

Osseetah Lake is busy, and the channel between Kiwassa Lake, was another busy place, clogged with motor craft. We peaked in and saw what we wanted to see and turned around. Lake Flower is more of the same before curving around and entering the town of Saranac Lake with its mandatory takeout and portage, around the dam.

VERMONT AND QUEBEC: 174 MILES

LAKE CHAMPLAIN AND ISLE LA MOTTE

Lake Champlain, or Pitawbagok as the Abinaki call it, sits along the northern New York, Vermont border, with the very northern section bumping itself into Canada, and at almost 500 square miles it's one of the largest lakes in the eastern United States.

The trail cuts across the lake from Plattsburg to South Hero Island, and works its way up through North Hero, to Hog Island and the Missisquoi National Wildlife Refuge on the Vermont mainland. In bad weather you can opt to take the Grand Isle Ferry to South Hero and work your way up the islands, but like any other big lake, you need to pay attention to the weather.

Paddling on Champlain can quickly change from a pleasant day of boating on the lake to something more akin to being caught on the ocean in a storm. The trail also

Lake Champlain.

Chazy Reef fossils.

includes Isle la Motte which sits to the west of North Hero Island and that's where we were headed; we wanted to check out the Goodsell Ridge Preserve. We were in luck the day we arrived to start our journey. The lake was flat calm under a sunny, windless day, an ideal boating day; and even though we did take advantage of the Grand Isle ferry crossing, we were able to get to Isle la Motte without any problems. After paddling up North Hero Island from Knight Point State Park, we stopped at the Pelots Point boat launch for lunch before crossing Horseshoe Shoals and landing at Holcomb Point where we took out our boats, to begin the short hike to the preserve. Ilse la Motte is a quiet slow-moving place, like a dead-end side street on a country road and we were taken aback by the pace: plodding, peaceful, quiet.

The preserve was as quiet as the Isle the day we visited. The large display barn was occupied by docents, but this was the kind of place we needed to explore on our own. It's the kind of site were people talk in whispers and walk along the trails with reverence, understanding they're walking on historic ground or I guess, prehistoric ground. We found many fossils, their outline pressed into the ancient rock; fossils of creatures that existed even before the earth had established dry land. Something I still can't wrap my head around. The Goodsell Preserve is part of the Chazy Fossil Reef, the oldest fossil reef on earth. The reef once located on the other side of the equator in the Iapetus Sea is 480 million years old—320 million years older than the age of the dinosaurs. The fossil record of the Chazy includes ancient corals; precursors of today's species, ancient sponges known as stromatoporoids, trilobites and cephalopods.

When we ended back at the barn, one of the docents explained about the Fisk Quarry down the road. It too is now protected, but when it was an active quarry, some stone block marketed as "black marble" was used to build the U.S. Capital Building and the National Gallery of Art in Washington D.C.

CLYDE RIVER

In August I took a solo trip to Vermont expecting a variety of safe paddles exploring the sections of the trail we'd missed in the spring. Little did I know, I'd experience some of the more challenging paddles of my journey.

My first paddle was a trip down the Clyde River exploring a section known as the Fen. Starting at the Ten-mile Square Boat Launch, the river weaves its way through a marshy swamp-like maze, that ends at "the Tubes," two large pipes running under Five Mile Square Road. The Fen is home to nesting ospreys and in addition to the actual paddle, photographing an osprey and other wildlife, was the goal.

The water was down but looked navigable, something I expected at this time of year. And even though the low water caused a steeper launch point than I remembered, the river's flow seemed lethargic, a good indication the paddle upriver, would be less strenuous than I'd previously thought. My goal was to make it through the Fen with as few issues as possible and with luck I'd photograph some interesting wildlife. If I made it all the way, I'd take a run through the Tubes before taking out at the Five Mile Square Road parking lot before walking back to get my car.

The Fens.

The Clyde River passing through
farmland north of the Fens.

Before launching I loaded my usual camera gear: Canon 80D SLR with a telephoto lens strapped to the forward deck in a waterproof bag, Canon 5D Mk II with wide-angle lens between my legs and under the forward deck in a dry bag, a waterproof Nikon automatic in the left pocket of my PFD, an Olympus Pen mirrorless camera in a waterproof casing on my lap and attached to the kayak with paracord, my cell phone in a waterproof case attached to the dashboard, and my Mavic Pro 2 drone in a waterproof case secured inside a dry bag and attached to the kayak's stern deck. Sounds like a lot but a photographer needs what he needs, and you never want to find yourself in a position to take a great shot and not have the proper equipment.

As I started up-stream I noticed the easiest paddling was in the deepest part of the riverway and used that information to follow the main channel, keeping my eyes and ears open for any wildlife. There were dead trees to my right, and one held a large osprey nest, but no osprey, still it was encouraging. Passing the Island of Dead Trees, I steered toward the right bank, not really a banking, but a wall of thick, dense, aquatic plants that surrounded almost everything in the Fen. Steering right wasn't as foolproof as I thought and I ended up in backwater dead ends a couple times, requiring me to retrace my course and try another direction. The paddling was going well, and I was getting some good pictures, and then it happened. I flipped my boat. I was sideways to the current admiring everything around me as the kayak drifted ever so slowly downstream when it bumped something just under the surface; a sunken piece of deadwood is what I thought, and I instinctively but also incorrectly swung my hips to look

The slow-moving Fens.

The Northern Forest Canoe Trail farm stand.

downstream as I leaned back, upstream; and that was it. The kayak rolled up further on whatever I'd bumped into and leaning in the wrong direction, I rolled my kayak over in less time that it took me to say "shit." I was in the water with my PFD pushed up but firmly in place. I could feel the bottom and was holding on to my boat's water-filled cockpit as I quickly looked around in panic, for of all things, my hat. I'd just dumped my boat with $15,000 in camera equipment and the thing I was concerned about most, was the wide-brimmed straw Stetson that Eric had bought me on a previous trip. Lost the paddle, retrieved the hat, rolled the boat back over and unable to bail it out, began the long journey back to the parking lot pushing the boat through the water. The hardest part was; the ever-changing depth of the water, no solid banking, the underwater snags I kept getting hung up on, and the realization that a kayak filled with water and gear has a mind of its own. Two hours and a few wrong turns later, I was back at the parking lot, and after dumping the water out and securing the kayak, I just laid down in the dirt parking lot, and waited for someone from the NFCT farm stand located just across the street, to come over and bring me an ice cream. They sell homemade ice cream sandwiches, and I was going to eat the one they brought me without even getting up off the ground; but no one came. I finally walked over, and the stand was empty, functioning under the honor system. Lucky for me I still had my wallet so with a couple wet dollars I was able to get my maple walnut ice cream bar.

I was lucky and not just because I didn't lose my hat. I was lucky because I'd been able to get out of my cramped cockpit stuffed with gear, when the boat rolled over. I was lucky none of my camera equipment was damaged, lucky all the drybags did their jobs. The camera I was holding when I flipped was a mirrorless digital in an underwater housing and I was able to retrieve it because it was tied to the kayak. I found my paddle a short way downstream, and when I finally got out of the water, I had most of the equipment I'd started with including my phone. But the lesson I came away with from this mess had nothing at all to do with luck, and everything to do with training and safety. When I rolled over, I had my PFD on, and it was properly zipped, clipped, and snugged up. Safety saves lives.

NULHEGAN RIVER

Day two promised to be hot and sunny, and I was excited to explore the Nulhegan. The Nulhegan River flows out of Nulhegan Pond in the town of Brighton, Vermont, but my first stop was to Brighton State Park and Island Pond. Island Pond's small park was just the place to have a quiet breakfast and hot coffee. I was reviewing my plan to kayak some of the Nulhegan River and needed an entry point. Logistics were on the light side and I had no option for a pickup, so the plan was to get on the river, and kayak my way downriver until I could get some good pictures. There are sections of the river with large bolder fields and rapids and I wanted to photograph some of it but not planning to run any of it, especially after the mess I'd found myself in on the Clyde the day before. The Nulhegan is remote in many places and it isn't the place to get hurt when you're alone, so I had two good reasons to find an access point, do some paddling, get the photos I wanted, and paddle back out.

The best spot for me was a turn off on Rt. 105. There was plenty of room to park and a sign welcoming; hunters, fishermen and kayakers to the Nulhegan and Silvio O. Conte National Wildlife Refuge. There was also a cut passageway toward the river.

I dropped the boat, loaded it with my gear and dragged it into the woods in search of the river which I thought I'd found only to realize after launching I was in an isolated section of water not navigable to the actual river. I was beginning to think this was a mistake but decided to reevaluate. I was too close to the river to turn back now, so I dragged the boat through the brush and water until I finally found the river. The danger in making decisions in a situation like this for a photographer is the tug one feels to get a great picture and that attraction sometimes outweighs common sense.

Once I found the river, I geared up the boat and positioned myself in the cockpit happy to have found calm water; it was flat, paddlable, and ripe for photography, but I quickly ran into a boulder field before I'd gone more than 100 yards and had to get out of the kayak. Boulder fields look great in pictures and this section in the early part of the year is nothing short of boiling rapids, now in midsummer it was more like a pile of rocks, so I walked my boat a short way through the field to photograph upstream. I walked a little further downstream thinking a longer field of rapids was an even better shot. It was, and I was feeling so good about the work I was doing, I walked further downstream shooting different angles and fields until I decided it was time to go back upstream and get out of the river, but I couldn't. I'd gone too far, and I was stuck. The water was flowing hard, the banks were steep, it was extremely difficult to walk upstream through the bolder strewn river while dragging a kayak full of

Island Pond.

Nulhegan boulder field.

The way out.

gear, and every time I stepped in a hole deeper than my waste, my PFD would have me bobbing around and heading back downriver. After a half hour of this nonsense I needed a new plan.

There were railroad tracks up above the banking on the left, but I had no idea if they crossed the road. They were also on the wrong side of the river. The other side was woods, steep woods, and I wasn't sure where I was in relation to the road so I decided to walk downriver a little further to see if things would improve and that's when I spotted what looked like a sign. When I got close enough, I could see it was a sign announcing I was on the Silvio O. Conte Preserve and lucky me, there was a riverside trail. Now I needed to figure out how to move everything up the hill. I pulled out all the camera gear, put my black kayak cover over the cockpit and stuck my kayak in the bushes. I kept my PFD on because it has a lot of things I might need; multi tool, first aid kit, compass, carabiner etc., and I strapped all my camera gear on. My drone pack with extra-long pack straps went on my back, drybag with SLR and long lens on top of the drone bag, and additional camera bag with mirrorless and second SLR strapped on my chest and clipped across my neck with a carabiner and parachute cord. The only other items I brought out of the woods were my keys and phone secured in a waterproof case and buttoned up in my fatigue pants, and of course my hat. Twenty agonizing minutes later I popped out of the woods and found myself at the northern headquarters building of the Silvio Conte on Route 105. Thankfully, my car was only three miles down the road and as long as I could walk—waddling like a duck is more accurate, three miles with all this "stuff" strapped on I was almost home free.

Connecticut River Kiosk.

I retrieved the car and drove back to the headquarters parking lot and for a few minutes I couldn't decide if I wanted to retrieve my kayak or just drive away. Retrieve sounds like an easy word, but the actual job of getting the kayak and the other gear up the hill was daunting. I "retrieved" it, and I can honestly say it wasn't as bad as I thought it would be; it was worse. There's no easy way to portage a kayak. You can't flip it upside down and place it on your shoulders. You can hang it off one shoulder like you see in the advertisements but not with half a boat full of gear, and anyway, the one-shoulder carry is good for about 50 feet. I got my boat up the hill by dragging it, and even that technique didn't work well. If you pick the nose up too high, the boat has a tendency to roll over, so the only way I made any real progress was by dragging it in a low crouch like a knuckle dragging Neanderthal, and that's what I did for the next two hours. When I finally got to the parking lot, I half expected to be reprimanded for dragging my boat through a wildlife preserve but no one came out to talk to me, and once I had the kayak strapped on the car and all the other stuff stowed, I wasted no time stripping down to a t-shirt and shorts, and getting out of the parking lot. I headed to the town of Bloomfield and Debanville's General Store for some pizza and coffee. The plan had been to put in at the kiosk behind the store and kayak some of the Connecticut River, with a chance to photograph the high cliffs downriver, but the way my luck was running, I'd probably end up stuck again with no way to paddle back, and have to drag my kayak through some farmers field all night. The Connecticut would need to wait for another day.

CANADA–LAKE MEMPHREMAGOG– THE GRAND PORTAGE

My trip to Canada and Lake Memphremagog was another solo trip. It started off a little crazy. I launched my kayak from a jogging trail along the lake, behind a line of stores in Newport, Vermont. I launched through the bushes and onto the water with the intention of paddling to Indian Point, but after five minutes of paddling in a heavy wind and contradictory if not entirely oppositional whitecaps, I decided to turn around and check out South Bay on the other side of the roadway, possibly exploring up the Clyde River to Clyde Pond but the water was just as choppy and contradictory on the other side. I decided to keep the kayak on the car after that, and head to Mansonville, Canada to check out Chemin Vallee Missisquoi, also known as the Missisquoi River, in Canada, and the Chemin Peabody known to paddlers of the Northern Forest Canoe Trail as the Grand Portage. With any luck I'd end my day at Perkins Landing on the Canadian side of Lake Memphremagog.

Just south of Mansonville I found the NFCT kiosk and the North Branch of the Missisquoi. The water was shallow but paddlable in a kayak and I started north but not for very long; shallow water, rocky sections and some low water rapids blocked my way. It was easier traveling south but my goal was to the north, so I took out and headed to a place on the map called the Diorio Access. I didn't want to actually paddle, I wanted to find a place to park near the start of the Grand Portage; the 6-mile portage from Mansonville to the lake. Parking was tight, but I found a spot off the road, next

The start of the Grand Portage.

Lake Memphremagog.

to a farmer's field and started my walk. To be honest, until that moment, I hadn't used my portage wheels, and I wanted to see what they could do. They worked great but after two miles the portage became less flat and open, and started to become real work. It was time for me to decide what I really wanted to do, and it wasn't a hard decision.

I turned around and walked the two miles back to my car, strapped the kayak on the roof and headed for Perkins landing where I put the boat in for a little trip around the lake. It was flat calm up on this end and I had a relaxing paddle on a day that was filled with tension, partly because I was planning on the fly, all day. My biggest issue

The Mansonville NFCT Kiosk.

the whole trip besides not being able to see any of the petroglyphs on the farm stones along the portageway, was the sign I missed at the Perkins Landing parking lot. They were about to tow my car because I hadn't paid to park.

When I got back to the landing, they had my car hooked up and were preparing to leave. Worse than that, they were arguing with me in French. Luckily, they took my car off the truck, and let me go. After that it was a quick stop at Jewett's General Store up the street and back to the U.S. This was one of those days when it felt like I'd done a lot of work with not a lot of success. Maybe my list was too big and in hindsight I think it was. Next time I'll do more with less and see how that goes. Once back in Vermont I realized I was still hungry, I hadn't had breakfast and ate my sandwich in the car on the drive back, so I pulled into Martha's Diner in Coventry Vermont for breakfast in the afternoon before heading back to camp. The one lesson I did learn from all of this, is that I'm not a solo kind of guy. I don't plan on doing this alone again; I don't find the same satisfaction.

NEW HAMPSHIRE: 72 MILES

The water on the Upper Ammonoosuc was high but not as high as it had been in earlier weeks considering the amount of detritus hanging up in the strainers laying across our path. Strainers are trees that have fallen into the river, a byproduct of bank erosion, and they're a potential danger to anyone on the river—in or out of a canoe, because like a sieve, they strain out objects including people who happen to fall overboard. Nature's flotsam lodged in the branches of these trees hung as high as five feet in the air giving us a surreal image of the water's previous height; surprising, but not other-worldly, considering this serpentine river winds its way through a wide lowland floodplain, that drains snowmelt from the surrounding hills of the White Mountain's National Forest.

We were paddling downriver in the rain this spring morning, as water-soaked clouds moved back and forth from one side of the valley to the other, picking up moisture

Navigating the low-hanging trees on the Upper Ammonoosuc River. Many of these have submerged sections of trees that can be dangerous to canoeists.

Beaver activity along the river.

Eric takes a turn in the bow on our spring paddle on the Upper Ammo.

as they bumped into the surrounding hillsides, and like a pinball, rolled back across the lowlands to deliver it directly on top of us. We were wet, cold, and mud covered; thank God we think this is fun. There were signs of beaver activity, the half-gnawed base of riverside trees littered the high banks, although we didn't encounter any dams or lodges. We did see lots of ducks, and at one point a pair of geese putting up a constant argument, they stayed just ahead of us, squawking loudly as if leading us downriver in some strange parade. After a few bends in the river, they suddenly flew up and circled back to where we'd first met them and it occurred to me, they'd purposely lead us away from something, probably their nesting site; smart birds. Continuing our trek downriver, the sandbars that pester boaters in summer months, requiring them to drag their boats in shallow water, could be seen three or four feet below the surface. Watching the water as it flowed over the silty bottom, gave us a perspective of the power of this slow moving waterway as its volume of water dragged itself and everything it came in contact with, to its outflow with the Connecticut River, and in turn to the sea; raw kinetic energy in its purest form.

The more we paddled the harder it rained and since we'd put in at West Milan, by the time we closed in on the village of Stark we were thoroughly wet, with a considerable amount of rainwater sloshing around in the bottom of our boat. Approaching the whitewater just above the town, we saw the takeout for Stark on river left and steered for it, not wanting to run the bolder field. This wasn't the time to dump our gear and ourselves into the river, it was time for lunch.

After taking out, we visited the town of Stark whose crossroads is quintessential New England or more accurately, the romanticized version of a quaint New England town, with its white church, covered bridge, grange building and historic inn. Originally named Percy, it was renamed Stark after General John Stark who came up with the words that became New Hampshire's motto, "Live Free or Die." During World War II the town was also home to Camp Stark a German Prisoner of War Camp, where POWs worked in the surrounding forests supplying pulp wood for the mills in the neighboring town of Berlin.

Takeout before the rapid at the village of Stark, NH.

The Route 110 portage from the Upper Ammonoosuc to the Androscoggin; soft shoulder, narrow and hilly.

There's a Northern Forest Canoe Trail Kiosk located across the street from the river near the Grange building where you can sign in, and after working around the bolder field located north of the covered bridge, you can put in again. If you continue south, you'll need to portage again around two dams located in Groveton before the Upper Ammonoosuc meets up with the Connecticut River outside of town.

The portage from the Upper Ammonoosuc in West Milan to the Androscoggin River is about 4 miles and follows along Route 110A, a narrow, winding, hilly road, with a narrow sandy shoulder along each side; not a road we wanted to walk on, so we portaged again with our Ford pickup truck.

THE ANDROSCOGGIN

The water part of the trail picks up again, on the Androscoggin River at the Paul Bofinger Conservation Area boat launch and moves upriver towards the town of Errol. For us though it was important to head south of the trail's put-in to "The City That Trees Built" Berlin, New Hampshire; the former headquarters of the Brown Paper Company, at one time, one of the biggest paper companies in America.

The Androscoggin is 178 miles long and flows from its headwaters near Lake Umbagog, on the Maine, New Hampshire border before eventually emptying into the Atlantic Ocean near Brunswick, Maine. The history of the river is forever intertwined

The Androscoggin River from the air at Berlin showing the boom piers, some of the last remaining evidence of the North Woods former log drives.

Checking out the boom piers.

with North Woods lore and was once one of the main thoroughfares for mill and pulp logs headed to Berlin.

All winter long men and animals worked in the woods cutting, hauling and stacking logs close to frozen rivers and lakes in preparation for spring when ice out would signal the biggest ballet of the great north woods; the log drive. Log drives involved thousands of players from the infamous rivermen to line cooks, animal caretakers, mechanics, and plant workers.

The Brown Paper Company established a mill on the banks of the Androscoggin and began turning pulp logs into paper in the mid-1800s. Saw logs—long logs for lumber, had ceased coming downriver, replaced by pulp logs for paper. Pulp logs are cut in 4-foot lengths, much more efficient all around, and they were floated downriver to the big paper mills in Berlin.

As a kid, I travelled through Berlin every June on an annual fishing trip to Errol, and Berlin was one of those towns you could smell long before you saw it. The paper mill ran 24/7 producing pulp for paper production and in the process gave off an odor that smelled a lot like rotting cabbage; a smell that permeated everything. The visual experience however was extraordinary. The mill sat in the middle of the river, its stacks billowing yellowish brown smoke and steam, as the mill noise mixed with the sounds of a bustling town and the river, creating what felt like a cacophony of living energy. The eastern shoreline was filled with huge piles of logs, long logs that had been trucked to the paper plant; the new transportation process gearing up to replace the traditional log drive. The river was also lined with large wooden boxes; piers anchored with stone ballast, and put in place to keep order out of what looked like chaos. Booms and piers assisted with traffic control as the massive drive of logs closed in on the mill.

Today the mills are closed, most if not all the buildings have been dismantled for scrap; the fields across the river that once held countless cords of pulp wood are empty, and nature is slowly recapturing the land. The boom logs have gone the way of everything else, and are now just memories, but there is one lasting vestige of this once proud industry. The boom piers anchored to the riverbed stand as silent sentinels to a closed chapter of the proud history of the north wood's forest industry.

We launched on the other side of the river near the little league field and boat ramp to do a little exploring. After passing through this town and staring at the "Andro" all these years, I wanted to get out on this sleeping waterway and check out the piers. The water was smooth and so slow you had the feeling it wasn't moving until you stopped paddling and felt the gentle but strong tug as the river pulled itself and anything else, slowly and inexorably toward the giant orange floats, signaling the danger zone before the dam. We paddled to the piers and noticed the wood structures just below the surface. They're still intact, sitting, waiting.

The river is still an impressive reminder of what once made this city great, a symbol of the strength and resolve of the people who made the north country strong, and we feel fortunate to have paddled even just a little of this powerful waterway.

An hour later we loaded up and headed for the Pontook Reservoir to continue our paddle. The reservoir boat launch would allow us to bypass the lower rapids near Holt

The frozen Pontook Reservoir.

Hill but much to our surprise, the reservoir was still frozen over with end of winter, slushy looking, white ice, so we pushed on, past the 13-Mile Woods, home to numerous Class II rapids, and headed for Errol, NH.

ERROL

Errol is a trail town and a place I once pilgrimaged to each June to fish for trout and the elusive landlocked salmon. Back then it was a sleepy crossroads town with a few houses, camps, a catholic church, and a few municipal buildings radiating out from its center. There was also a rooming house, a general store and a diner. Not much has changed since those trips in the 1970s except L.L. Cote outfitters, a large sporting goods store in the center of town. The irony of the L.L. in the store's name didn't escape us and a visit inside impressed us with the amount and variety of gear. They have anything and everything you'd need for a trip on the water, and I believe Leon Leonwood would have been equally impressed if he'd had the chance to stroll the store's aisles.

One place we never miss when we visit Errol is the Errol General Store. The owner's homemade sandwiches and cookies are superb.

HEADING TO MAINE

We launched just above the dam at the Androscoggin River Boat Access and headed upstream toward Sweat Meadows and the entrance to Umbagog Lake. Paddling against the current was easy, the deep water and upstream breeze almost propelling us northward. I couldn't help but think as we cruised upriver how easy a day we were going to have, topped off with an easy paddle back to our truck. Little did I know, the trip back down river would test me, pushing me close to the breaking point. Umbagog is a shallow-water lake fed by the Rapid, Magalloway, and Dead Cambridge Rivers. It's the headwaters of the Androscoggin River and home to the Umbagog National Wildlife Refuge. The lake has close to thirty campsites scattered around its shoreline although most are located at the southern end of the lake and not in line with the water trail. The most important campsites for those on the NFCT are located in the Sunday Cove area near the mouth of the Rapid River and close to the portage takeout for the Carry Road.

We were paddling a circle route from the Errol dam to Umbagog to fish and explore, and all was going as planned until the wind picked up. The lake is susceptible to wind blowing north from the New Hampshire side of the lake, and when it started to blow in the late afternoon, we put our rods away and paddled for the river. We were paddling into a headwind, and as we approached the river the wind seemed to intensify, blowing our canoe sideways, backwards, left, right; any direction except the one we were paddling. Our canoe was a river canoe without a keel, and we resembled a sailboat without a rudder with two frustrated and exhausted paddlers on board. Entering the river's mouth, the wind intensified again in strength and sound. It was screaming at us across a frothing white capped sea. It wasn't a river anymore; it was a monster.

The Androscoggin River above the
Errol Dam during quiet times.

The Androscoggin River as it approaches
Unbagog Lake near Sweet Meadows.

The Andro with the wind-up and blowing a gale creating dangerous conditions.

We moved river left and tried paddling close to shore, at least we were out of the unobstructed blow in the middle, and we could mark our progress by the trees and bushes on the banking. Our progress became turtle like; paddle like crazy for 10 or 12 minutes to gain 4 or 5 feet, hold on to whatever shoreline vegetation you could get your hands on, rest 5 minutes, and then paddle like crazy for 10 or 12 minutes as we repeated the process over and over. Hours later, the landing in sight, we noticed a distinct line in the water; on the right was the blowing wind and white-capped water, on the left it was flat calm. The wind was still running up and over the Errol dam before jetting upriver toward the lake, but the landing located in a small cove and protected from the blow, didn't even have a ripple. I could see now that we'd make it back, and that's when my mood took a strange twist. In the middle of this blowing mess, I functioned with great determination and strong will, but once our destination was in front of us and reachable, I became frustrated and mad; upset at the river, upset at the trees, upset at the canoe, upset at everything that hadn't cooperated. And then I became upset with myself. I'd forgotten the message; nature doesn't like or dislike, feel bad, play favorites, or have a lesson plan; all that stuff is up to me. Lesson re-learned, and it would be a valuable lesson for me, before Eric and I completed our journey.

Unanticipated ice on Unbagog in late spring.

MAINE: 347 MILES

RETURN TO UMBAGOG

In late May of the following year we returned to Umbagog, this time from the southern end, only to find the lake iced in. The days and weeks leading up to our trip had been sunny and warm, and it surprised us to find most of the lake except about 100 feet along the shoreline, icebound. Eric suggested we launch and use the canoe as an icebreaker and see how far that would take us, but my guess was not far, so we decided to just sit back and enjoy ourselves in the moment. And considering the canoeing of the last few days, a quiet moment sitting on the banking, soaking up the rays of a hazy spring sun, seemed like a great idea. So, we ripped up our schedule, left the canoe on the truck, and sat down to soak up the view. What a difference from the last time we'd visited; a time when the wind blew hard enough to disturb rational thinking.

A bald eagle soared overhead to the west in lazy counterclockwise circles, slowly increasing and then decreasing its flightpath, while closer to the ground, the first insects of spring buzzed around, possibly as bewildered as us about the view. Sound travels a long distance under these conditions and someone in the distance, possibly far to the north was cutting wood, reminding us of Umbagog's rich history as part of the timber industry. The lake was part of the Brown Paper Company's log highway that fed the mills in Berlin to the south each spring; first for saw logs and later pulpwood. The lake is also home to smallmouth bass, a fish threatening one of the premier fishing destinations in America: the Rapid River.

THE RANGELEY LAKES REGION

Heading north, the trail from Umbagog Lake to Lower Richardson is a portage that runs along a usually smooth carry road, and as portages go this one is uneventful, but the uniqueness and history of this small corner of Maine is worth a few words. The 3 ½ mile Rapid River that empties into Unbagog Lake parallels the carry road, and is considered a magic place for trout fishermen who pilgrimage to this sacred spot every year. One of the few places left with a pure strain of native brook trout and landlocked salmon. A place where fly-fishing rules the day and turns the dreams of grown men into a Huckleberry Finn quest. The Rapid River, Pond-in-the-River and the pools of pocket waters that own the bottom of Middle Dam have the magic power to turn men to boys. This part of Maine is also known for some of the Maine Wood's strongest women; author Louise Dickinson Rich, fly tier Carrie Stevens, and Fly Rod Crosby are all part of local history and lore.

Pushing your canoe along the carry road will bring you to another magic place; Forest Lodge. Forest Lodge is on the National Register of Historic Places and is the Maine home of Louise Dickinson Rich, author of *We Took to the Woods*, the autobiography of her life in Maine's backwoods. Here are a few words from her book describing her surroundings:

Between two ranges of mountains, the Boundary Mountains and the Blue Mountains, lie a high wild valley, the basin that holds the Rangeley Lakes. The country is crisscrossed with ridges, dotted with swamps and logans, and covered with dense forest. I like to think of the lakes coming down from the North of us like a gigantic staircase to the sea. Kennebago to Rangeley to Cupsuptic, down they drop, level to level, through short, snarling rivers; Mooselukmeguntic to the Richardsons to Pond-in-the-River, and through Rapid River to Umbagog, whence they empty into the Androscoggin and begin the long Southeasterly curve back to the ocean. I like to say their names, and I wish I could make you see them.

—Louise Dickinson Rich, We Took to the Woods, 1942

Louise's typewriter and book collection.

Interior of the Summer House at Forest Lodge.

The Rapid River with Forest Lodge's summer house on its left, at center.

Sport fishing the famous Rapid River.

Lower Richardson at dawn.

Forest Lodge is home to the Summer House and Winter House. The winter house was insulated and warmer than the summer house, but the Summer House is the real gem; once described as "a living, disappearing part of Maine history on a river of nationally recognized ecological and fly-fishing significance."

Passing Forest Lodge, you eventually arrive at Middle Dam on Lower Richardson Lake; the end of your portage for this section of the trail. Just to the left of the dam keepers house is Lakewood Camps, one of the oldest sporting camps in Maine. Sequestered in the unorganized territories of the Maine Woods, there are only three ways to get to this sports camp; portaging from Umbagog like us, flying in by floatplane from Rangeley, or boating over from South Arm on the far end of the lake. The cabins decorated with an eclectic array of mismatched furniture are stretched out in a

The big one, the elusive trout.

row on a low rise above the shore and the main lodge with office and dining room is off to the left. If you're looking for a place to stay for a few days or weeks were you can put the rest of the world on hold, this is the place.

The Upper and Lower Richardsons are deep-water lakes that were melded together with the construction of Upper Dam. For canoeists, wind is the concern on this section of the trail. Whitecaps during a blow are not unusual as a long unimpeded wind can drive down the lake increasing in speed, as it funnels through and down the mountain ranges located on both sides.

Another woman who rose to popularity and fame not far from The Richardsons was Cornelia Thurza Crosby, better known as Fly Rod Crosby. She was the first registered Maine Guide; an interesting achievement in a field dominated by men. She was also a writer who helped publicize the advantages of traveling to Maine's Rangeley area to fish and hunt. She was probably the reason many of the "sports" that traveled to Maine were women; as eager as men to enjoy the outdoors with all its offerings. Fly Rod was a tireless promoter of Maine's outdoor activities both in her writings and as an exhibiter in sportsman's expositions. She was surely a role model for young women, as a strong, independent individual, leading by example and demonstrating the possibility of unlimited potential.

Rangeley Lake and region has been a trout fishing mecca for over 150-years, ever since word got out about the trophy size brook trout that live in the lake. Sports, people of means from large cities to the south, flocked to the region to try their hand at fishing. And taking care of the rapidly increasing number of sports that found their way to Rangeley helped develop a new cottage industry. Sports camps and hotels increased in number and size, the Maine Guide service was organized, and a new type of craft—the Rangeley boat, was developed to assist both sports and guides in their pursuit of the big one.

Eric and I headquartered at Rangeley Lake State Park, and paddled and fished to reckless abandon in shallow coves and deep, cold-water pockets from one end of the lake to the other, and as much as we pursued him, the big one we were looking for is still hiding somewhere.

We spent 5 days at Rangeley in June, and traveled mostly by canoe, exploring the lake and water's edge. The clear water is what I remember most. It's one of those places were the clarity of the water is so pure it almost makes it invisible in photographs.

Early morning paddles for us were the best. The wind was usually calm, the lake's surface was flat, and the rain held off. Most of our time was spent searching for loons, and they abound in the area. They put us to sleep at night with their eerie calls, especially their wailing call, as they interacted in the darkness with their mate and others.

If you read the section on portaging you already know the craziness and polar opposite of the Rangeley portage compared to those that must be endured in the wilderness, so we aren't going to repeat it here. What is worth repeating are the water conditions on the Dead River once you've paddled and portaged beyond Rangeley. We've never found this part of the trail very paddleable and the best thing we can say

Rangeley sunset, looking west toward
Mooselukmeguntic Lake.

about portaging along Route 16 is that it's dangerous. As section paddlers our plan for this part of the trail was and is simple. We again loaded up our truck and portaged our way to Flagstaff Lake in two-wheel drive.

MOOSE RIVER AND MOOSEHEAD LAKE

Paddling the Moose River was a breeze this time, but I really need to pay attention. A few years ago, they opened the dam creating a whole new environment; fast water, foam, strong currents, and hidden obstacles; make sure your PFD is zipped and snapped.

Moving off the river and on to Moosehead Lake for me has always been a turbulent experience. It must have something to do with wind and conflicting currents. Just another place to hold on to your hat.

Moosehead at 117 square miles of water, is a very big lake, and because it's big, lots of other things happen in a big way including; boat traffic, plane traffic, and the

Brassua Lake with whitecaps and a blowing wind. We called it a day.

Maynards Sports Camp located on the Moose River in Rockwood.

always and inevitable wind. When Thoreau crossed the lake with his guide, the wind was a challenge:

Again we crossed a broad bay opposite the mouth of Moose River, before reaching the narrow strait at Mount Kineo, made what the voyageurs call a traverse, and found the water quite rough. A very little wind on these broad lakes raises a sea which will swamp a canoe.

When the wind is aft, and not too strong, the Indian makes a spritsail of his blanket. He thus easily skims over the whole length of this lake in a day.

The Indian paddled on one side, and one of us on the other, to keep the canoe steady, and when he wanted to change hands he would say "t'other side." He asserted, in answer to our questions, that he had never upset a canoe himself, though he may have been upset by others.

Think of our little eggshell of a canoe tossing across that great lake, a mere black speck to the eagle soaring above it!

Moosehead Lake is a busy place
with lots of traffic and weather.

The Moose River on a slow flow from the dam at Brassua Lake to Moosehead Lake.
Maynard's in Maine, an old-time sports camp is across the river to the left, and you can see
Mt. Kineo in the distance. Kineo is made of volcanic rock that boiled out of the earth, rising
over 700 feet creating impressive vertical cliffs. The rock is called Kineo "flint" but it's not

actually a true flint, it's a rhyolite hornstone. Hot volcanic magma boiled up and exploded onto the surface where it cooled creating the largest deposit of Kineo "flint" in the world. Native Americans traveled long distances to collect this stone for producing arrowheads, hatchets, and other tools.

KINEO

We were lucky. We canoed this water in the early morning hours of 2 summer days, and the lake was as flat as glass with no wind, not even a breeze, like ice skating; an exception to the rule for this big body of water. We took a break from paddling to follow Thoreau up Mt. Kineo. The view is majestic from the fire tower that sits at the top, and it allows a perspective of the massiveness of the lake that cannot be

understood from the water's edge. The mountain is a huge peninsula of rhyolite with 700-foot vertical cliffs; an igneous magmatic rock, it usually forms when molten larva breaks the surface of the earth and cools. Kineo's rock formation is often called flint, but it's actually a type of hornstone that has the characteristics of flint making it a prized position of early Native Americans who used it to make; arrow heads, hatchets and other tools.

The view of Moosehead Lake looking
north toward the Northeast Carry,
from the summit of Mt. Kineo.

NORTHEAST CARRY

We arrived at the Northeast Carry just in time for muffins. The Carry is home to Raymond's Country Store—a true oasis in the middle of the Maine Woods and Shirley who owns the store with her husband Ed, had just removed her home-made muffins from the oven. We needed to resupply, but as far as the muffins were concerned, we had to wait a few, because Shirley wouldn't allow us to eat them until they'd cooled enough to sell. Shirley has that dry, straight faced sense of humor you find in Maine, and the discussion we were having started to turn into a game show while we waited for our muffins to cool down. Besides the muffins we needed to resupply some of our food but as I reached for a package of rolls, Shirley told us we couldn't buy the bread; the more I pointed at the stocked shelf, the more she said, "Nope, you can't have that." She finally explained that her brand name bread was out of date and possibly not 100%. She was about to put bread in the oven and told us to wait for her homemade, but we needed every minute that day for kayaking on the West Branch of the Penobscot, Lobster Stream, and Lobster Lake, so she gave us the moldy bread for free and sent us on our way, but not before giving us one more tidbit. She said a man had come through not that long ago, determined to paddle the entire Northern Forest Canoe Trail on a paddle board. I was amazed and asked how he was when he arrived at the Carry. Shirley stated with a straight face; "Well, by the time he got to us, it seemed like all the fun was drained out of it." Plain and simple. Thank you, Shirley and Ed, and as soon as we can, we'll be back for a loaf of homemade.

Moosehead is still littered
with the remains of its days
as a logging highway.

Lobster Lake has some good examples of volcanic rocks—igneous rock that formed when molten rock cools and solidifies. The lake also has great examples of an interwoven limestone/mudstone rock structure that show varying degrees of erosion, creating a ribbed effect. This example below is at Ogden Point where we set up our camp.

LOBSTER LAKE

Lobster Stream is a 2-mile paddle between the lake of the same name and the West Branch of the Penobscot River. It has a large parking lot complete with an NFCT kiosk, and for good reason. Paddling and exploring Lobster Lake and stream is a spectacular experience. The stream is home to beaver, muskrats, moose and waterfowl,

along with an assortment of flora and fauna. The stream is also subject to a dynamic flow and can run into the lake, or out of the lake, depending on the water level in the West Branch of the Penobscot.

We pushed off under a warm sun that beat off the water. I cruised along the left shore in shade looking for wildlife as Eric paddled more to the center. I tend to straggle a little behind because of the need to pull out and then re-secure the camera gear every time I photograph, making Eric who's usually paddling ahead, the "advance man" looking and spotting things of interest; so he was the first to see the big guy. There was a moose foraging on water plants close to the stream. It was a bull sporting a crown of half-developed felt-covered antlers, chomping away on aquatic greens. I was surprised to see him considering all the canoe and kayak traffic running up and down the stream. I guess he was hiding in the bushes, waiting for boats to go past before jumping back in to eat.

Lobster Lake is impressive. It has a long sandy beach in one section that rivals many beaches on Cape Cod, and interesting geological structures; evidence of igneous rock formations that occurred when magma from deep in the earth, bubbled up to the surface, and cooled. We ate lunch sitting on a sandy beach next to a rock that in contrast looked like it had just oozed out of the ground and solidified on the spot.

MOOSE

Moose are the tallest mammals in North America and Maine has more moose than any other State along the trail with a population of about 75,000. They're plant eaters and because of their large size—an average moose weighs about 800 lbs; they eat up to 100 lbs a day. They eat a variety of different plant material including shoots from

Maine moose.

Young bull moose on Lobster Stream.

young trees and some grasses. They're fond of aquatic plants and can be found feeding along riverbanks and in shallow sections of ponds and lakes. The four moose we spotted in the past two years were all eating aquatic plants. They also need sodium and are often spotted along roadways licking salt off the road in springtime.

They are strange looking gangly animals with long legs holding a large body including an elongated head. If they need to run on a hard surface like a paved road, they demonstrate a strange gait and move like they're on ice; no control. But don't be fooled if you bump in to one in the woods. They can run faster than a person and if provoked, will charge. I read a statistic that said moose kill more people annually than black bears, but I have the feeling that statistic includes car accidents.

Moose are said to be solitary animals; I suppose if you need to eat between 75 and 100 lbs. of food a day you aren't going to hang around in large groups. The most common setting of moose together is usually a female with her calf. Moose usually give birth to a single calf but can give birth to twins.

ALLAGASH

The Allagash Wilderness Waterway has coexisted with the timber industry and others for centuries, and after it was declared a wilderness waterway in 1966, the State of Maine has worked tirelessly to maintain a regulatory balance between three competing interests; industry, public accessibility and the philosophy of wilderness. And nothing demonstrates that more than the Allagash Wilderness Waterway (AWW) rules and regulations. There are rules that stipulate all sorts of things including how wide a canoe and a kayak can be in relation to its length. There are rules that exclude certain kinds of equipment; rules about where you're allowed to pitch a tent, and rules about where you can park your car. There are also rules for cutting timber. Loggers must make sure they don't cut close to the waterway and are required to maintain what's come to be known as "the beauty strip."

Dragonflies were everywhere on the lower sections of the Allagash, especially during our time on Chamberlain Lake where they landed on my kayak and sometimes on my kayak paddle as I was stroking along, jumping off as I dipped the paddle into the water.

The Beauty Strip.

The woods in early morning after a rainstorm as seem from the river's edge.

Canoeists enjoying a fall paddle along
the Allagash Wilderness Waterway.

A beauty strip is a Restricted Zone created to maintain the appropriate visual experience and feel of being on a wilderness adventure. This means no commercial cutting within 400 to 800 feet of the waterway. Like a curtain on a stage, the beauty strip hides the actors from the audience although in some cases I'm not sure which is which.

To be honest, I have no issue with the rules and okay with the idea of accessibility as long as they don't start installing elevators at the campsites and sidewalks along the dirt roads, but I do find some rules humorous and downright funny when taken out of context; almost as funny as learning that the Rangers mow the lawns at all the remote campsites on the Allagash. The idea of seeing a ranger in his canoe with his lawn mower and gas can seem somewhat hilarious especially when I think about the possibility of being woken up in the morning not by the sounds of a wild animal but rather by the sound of someone mowing my wilderness lawn.

When talking about watercraft the rules define what a canoe is and what a kayak isn't in relation to the AWW, so pay attention all you, homemade canoe and kayak builders. For canoes, the width of a canoe at its widest point cannot exceed more than 20% of its overall length, and the transom if there is one cannot exceed more than 26 inches in width. The measurements are made outside the hull but don't include gunwales, rub rails of spry rails. Kayaks at their widest point cannot measure more than 25% of the boat's overall length; our kayaks which are wide because we need a stable platform for photography made it under the wire by 1 inch. If you're bad at math no worries, they provide a chart with maximum sizes.

It's also against the rules for more than 12 people to go on a canoe trip together. If you have more than 12 in your group, you must divide up into smaller groups which makes sense, however you must canoe in a way as not to be seen by each other. The rules say; the groups must canoe at least one-half mile apart, can't stay at the same campsite, and can't share equipment. If you must split your group up, make sure you split up the matches, food, and toilet paper, or one group might have a much better experience than the other.

THE LOWER ALLAGASH

We arrived at the Telos Road checkpoint at 9:40 in the evening, 10 minutes after closing, although the building was lit up like a Christmas tree, and we were happy to find out we could register and pay using a remote phone/camera system. This allowed us to drive to the Chamberlain Bridge launch site at the Telos Cut and sleep for a few hours in darkness as we waited for dawn to arrive. And it was dark. We were in a place with no artificial illumination for miles and with no moon in sight and only stars in the sky, something could have pressed its face against the windshield, and we might not have seen it. Up at 4:00am we started unpacking, and none too soon, we'd been in the truck since 2:00 the previous afternoon.

We spotted many bald eagles along the trail and observed at least one in every state we paddled. Once on the endangered species list, their populations have increased greatly over the past 40 years with estimates of well over 100,000 birds living in the United States and Canada today.

Our first animal sighting was in the early dawn hours of this hazy summer day, when a muskrat passed right in front of us; head down with eyes just above the surface, it cut a shallow vee across the mirrored surface.

Thoreau had also observed a muskrat when he visited Maine and he made the following observation:

Just before night we saw a musquash (he did not say muskrat), the only one we saw in this voyage, swimming downward on the opposite side of the stream. The Indian, wishing to get one to eat, hushed us, saying, "Stop, me call 'em "; and sitting flat on the bank, he began to make a curious squeaking, wiry sound with his lips, exerting himself considerably. I was greatly surprised, thought that I had at last got into the wilderness, and that he was a wild man indeed, to be talking to a musquash! I did not know which of the two was the strangest to me. He seemed suddenly to have quite forsaken humanity, and gone over to the musquash side.

The term "Musquash" is most likely an Anglicized version of an Abinaki word for this animal, and the "muskrat" label a derivative of that, even though muskrats aren't members of the rat family; just big semi aquatic rodents fond of eating plants. They're also part of Native American creation narratives; viewed as the only animal able to swim to the bottom of the sea and bring up mud to help the creator build dry land.

Our earth-diver wasn't hauling up balls of mud, more likely he was cruising around in search of breakfast; looking for cover to hide from the bald eagles that circle this part of the lake; or heading home to its push-up. Built in swamps and marshland and constructed of mud and vegetation, push-ups include an underwater entrance, and can be up to three feet high. A dry mound in the middle of wetlands; maybe this is how the creation myth started.

We launched and kayaked along the Telos Cut into Chamberlain Lake. This is a lake known for dangerous winds that blow in a north/south direction with potential for dangerous whitecaps. We paddled on to a mirror lake, so flat the blue sky blending with the blue surface of the water was almost imperceptible. Eric headed toward the center of the lake chasing a pair of loons, while I ran inshore following a bald eagle that slowly circled the lake before landing in the high branches of a pine at the lakes edge; a great observation point for checking the water for movement.

Muskrat heading home.

Moving north we entered a cove. In lower water you can observe dead trees as Thoreau did, they seem to be everywhere. We only observed the higher branches as they protruded from the surface. We explored the large erratic that has sat here since the last great glacier receded north, it's so large there's a geological marker on its top. We made a half-hearted attempt to paddle up Mud Stream but no luck, there was too much debris blocking our entry. We were also convinced the present-day carry is as; buggy, obstructed, wet and dirty as it was when Thoreau portaged it in 1853, and Steele in 1880.

Back on the main part of the lake and across the water sits Nugent's, a historic sports camp only accessible by boat, and just north of Nugent's is the former site of Chamberlain Farm.

Chamberlain Farm, once a lifeline for the men, machinery and support animals of the 19th century logging industry that once dominated the Maine Woods is gone, and all that remains today are a few cellar holes. But in 1880 when Thomas Steele visited, things were very different:

Paddling in the cove of dead trees just above Mud Stream. We flew the drone off the giant erratic boulder in the cove.

Break for lunch.

The buildings are situated on a hill fronting the lake, and command a view of the greater part of the water. . . . During the summer months the products of the farm are gathered into the barns, and are used to feed the hundreds of "log drivers" who in the winter and spring are annually sent to this region. These "loggers" are a hardy set of men, receiving a dollar and a half a day when "on the drive," and work form 2 AM to 10 PM often exposed to great perils and the inclemency of the weather. Large herds of cattle and sheep are pastured here, and on the hill at the rear of the house I noticed a number of Mules.

We'd hoped to be able to look back in time and experience something of this place, to touch history or at least visualize it, but nature the great equalizer, and ultimate moderator of all things made by man, had reclaimed, obscured, or erased our footprint. Disappointed or not, we discovered there's still a place in the Maine Woods to satisfy our curiosity about Chamberlain Farm and other farms like it. So, we traveled over to check it out; its name is Pittston Farm.

Pittston Farm was built by Great Northern Pulp and Paper Company in 1907 at the intersection of the North and South Branches of the Penobscot River and functioned

as a farm until 1971. The 45-acre farm now on the National Register of Historic Places was built to supply the men and equipment including animals working in the winter woods, timbering for Great Northern's pulp mills.

The farm includes a boarding house, a 7-bay carriage house, a blacksmith shop with original equipment, and office building and three barns. One of the barns has been organized as a museum. The carriage house has been converted to rental units, and we ended up staying a couple nights. The highlight of our experience was eating dinner in the communal dining room; homemade, old school dining.

TRAINS

The northern end of Chamberlain Lake feels like a large disorganized wilderness museum with different exhibits scattered around to be explored and often puzzled over; not the least of which are two full size locomotives, and a long line of rotting box cars; remains of the Eagle Lake and West Branch Railroad.

Logging has always been a valuable commodity in the North Woods and men have gone to great lengths to make the industry work; some worked hard to make a living while others worked hard to make their fortunes. One audacious plan that worked for some years was to change the flow of at least three lakes and a couple rivers to bring logs away from Canadian interests in the north, redirecting them to the American market in the south. The Telos dam, Telos Cut and Lock Dam were all part of an enterprise to raise the level of water in Chamberlain Lake, to reverse the natural flow of the Allagash, sending logs south to Telos Lake, over the new dam and down through the newly built Cut to the East Branch of the Penobscot River. Logs would then float

Our first discovery indicating we were on the right "track" were the railroad tracks. We followed them back to the remains of the Eagle Lake and West Branch Railroad.

naturally downriver to be processed in Maine mills instead of mills in Canada. There was an additional financial incentive to make this happen. Logs passing through the Telos cut were assessed a fee their owners were required to pay to the dam owner.

The weak point in this operation was Lock Dam between Eagle and Chamberlain Lakes. It washed away and had to be rebuilt at least twice, but the real issue was the limited number of logs at a time, workers could get past the dam and into Chamberlain Lake.

In 1902 a tramway was constructed that pulled logs through the woods from the Eagle Lake side to Chamberlain Lake. The tramway had its problems but functioned for six years and when working efficiently it moved an estimated 500,000 board feet of lumber a day.

Replacing the tramway was the biggest project of all; the construction of the Eagle Lake and West Branch Railroad. In the winter of 1926, the entire railroad operation including two full-size locomotives, 25 box cars, and over 13 miles of track, were hauled through the woods and across frozen Eagle Lake to become the EL&WB Railroad. The 13-mile railroad included a 15,000-foot trestle over Allagash Stream. All of this was built to move logs from Eagle Lake to Umbazooksus Lake and on to the West Branch of the Penobscot.

For Eric and me, all this "stuff" in the woods had to be explored, but we hesitated to drag our kayaks and gear through the woods. There are two portages from Chamberlain to Eagle Lake; a one-tenth of a mile hike around the Lock Dam will bring you to Eagle Lake and a paddle around to the left will bring you to a small inlet were the locomotives are located. The second portage is a three-fourths-mile hike along the old tramway. We decided on option 3; a march through the wood along the train tracks once we located them.

Maps make it look easy but when you're bushwhacking through the woods in dense cover and variable terrain, it can be difficult. It was a hot, steamy, buggy day, and we were a little disoriented, so we started walking in circles; on purpose of course. It's a tactic we use to see if we can find a clue, any clue that'll give us a hint of our location, and we found one. Way off to one side we spotted something bright red attached to a tree. It was a marker for the "beauty strip" the no cut zone within 400 feet of the

These two locomotives, vestiges of the past, sit like sentinels in the woods next to Eagle Lake.

The largest relics are the tramway, train engines, and boxcars left in the woods near Eagle Lake. The tramway sits in the same location, trees growing in and around the once moving parts. The trains and boxcars of the Eagle Lake and West Branch Railroad rest in the woods in the same place they were parked in 1933 when the railroad shut down.

AWW; we were close to the lake; maybe. Facing the stick, we moved right and after bushwhacking for another 15 minutes we walked over a long knoll and found the tracks. Walking the tracks, we began to find other evidence; a railroad signal, boiler parts and switches, before rounding a corner and right before us, larger than life and sitting in the wilderness, were two huge locomotives. Even more impressive for me were the two lines of rotting box cars that occupied a long, wooded berm running parallel to the shoreline. We climbed on the trains like little kids and checked out other pieces to the puzzle including the old tramway. It was a fascinating time, and it put in perspective for us, just how innovative and determined the men were, who worked in these woods; loggers, and lumbermen; larger than life. No wonder the statue of Paul Bunyan in Bangor stands 31-feet tall.

Once we were done playing on all the stuff, we needed to follow the tracks back to Chamberlain and walk the lake to find our kayaks. After that, it was paddling, paddling, paddling.

Twentieth-century logging camps still stand in the woods today, the buildings slowly rotting away, no longer of service to the logging industry.

Paddling back.

THE UPPER ALLAGASH

"Stand against the fence please and stay in front of the truck" was the request from the Canadian Border Patrol officer. It was the second time he'd said that to me and upon reflection I guess it wasn't a request, it was more like an order. We'd spent the last three days and nights on the Allagash accompanied by on-again off-again rain, including some impressive downpours leaving us and most of our equipment; wet, moldy and smelly. As trips go, it was a classic and one of our best of the year, but at this point we were more than ready to put on some dry clothes, and because the nearest clothing store was across the river, we headed to Canada. The two Border patrol officers who'd come out to welcome us to Canada, were now going through our gear, digging items out of pockets and pouches, searching through mess kits and rooting through bags of wet clothing. I was fine with all of this until the guy on my side of the truck started pulling out my camera gear including my drone. He was currently trying to dislodge the drone's hard case from its waterproof backpack by shaking it out onto the ground; not something you should be doing in front of a photographer, and the reason I pushed my luck and stepped around to the side of the truck again. I just couldn't help myself. I needed to tell him again to be careful with the camera equipment.

When they were done digging through things, the officer on my side came around to show me the knives he'd discovered; one from a pocket on my PFD, the other out of my backpack. He wanted to let us know it was illegal to bring knives into Canada that could be opened by flicking your wrist, and he began demonstrating by doing a

No wonder they stopped us.

lot of hard flicking with mine. As he flicked away with abandon, I began to feel sorry for him; he was expending a lot of energy with no success, it was like watching a young child trying to demonstrate how to do a pushup but unable to get off his knees, so I reached inside my jacket and pulled out my big folding survival knife encouraging him to give it a try. I was silently rooting for him as he began flicking away, but he was again, unsuccessful. I felt sorry for him all over again, even a little embarrassed, until he abruptly stopped. He handed me back my knives, and it was over; passports returned, we were told we could go, so we got in the truck and headed to as they say in Canada, "The Walmart."

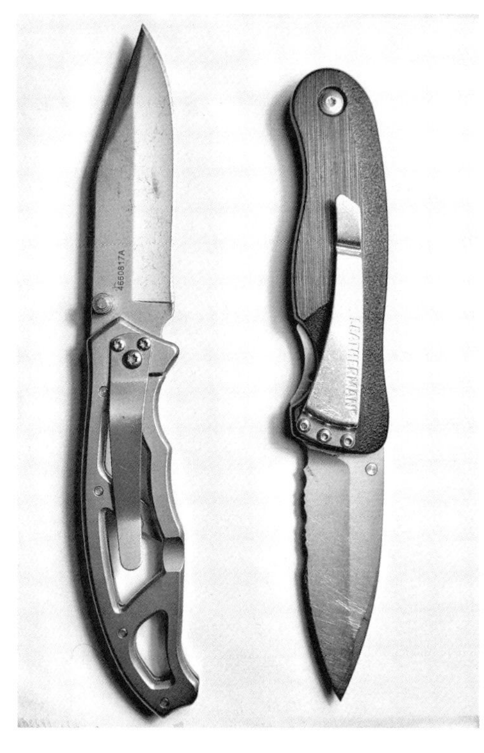

After buying dry clothes, we returned to the border and entered US Customs where the US Border Patrol decided they'd search our stuff too but with a twist. We were told to pull around behind the building, park the truck in one of the inspection bays and bring all our purchases inside. The building is a no cell phone zone so we placed our phones into a box and an officer began going through our purchases looking for of all things, clothing made in China, and if our China-made goods totaled over $200, we were told we'd be paying a federal tariff for importing Chinese goods into the United States. Most of or new clothes were made by someone named "George" who'd stenciled his name inside each item including my pair of $12 shoes, and I'd guessed correctly, he worked in China, so we were bracing for yet another fee on our already fee-filled trip, but we came in just under the wire. Happy with the news, we collected our dry clothes and prepared to leave until the agents announced they were going to inspect our truck, and we were told to take a seat. Twenty minutes later they let us go with one piece of advice. The next time we brought a drone into Canada and crossed back into the States, we should carry some form of documentation showing it was ours to avoid complications. I guess it wasn't enough that our FAA registration number was stenciled on the drone's body.

As we drove away, I couldn't help but think it might have been easier for us if we'd just bought the Halloween costumes we saw at the Fort Kent Dollar Store and worn them home. It might have been easier, it definitely would have taken less time, but I suppose if we'd been stopped by law enforcement on the ride back to Massachusetts, we'd be going through some other type of inspection. I also realized the US must have a more lenient policy on knives you could open with a flick of the wrist, since none of the US Customs officers had engaged in any form of knife flicking competition.

We stopped in Portage, Maine, for the evening and after; a shower, dry clothes, a room with beds, a hot meal, and oh yes, ice cream, we felt the little remaining energy we'd mustered on this final day just drain away. We were officially exhausted.

I spend some of my time just staring at the ceiling, but I also reflected on just how great this final trip was. We'd packed so much into it and had been going non-stop since Wednesday afternoon. My body was exhausted, but my mind was still on over-drive. What I needed to do was slow down the mental motor and reflect. And so, I did.

Our upper Allagash trip began in Eric's backyard on a bright sunny September day where I found myself sitting with his chickens. We were all waiting for him to get home from work; all thirteen of us, the chickens wanting to be fed and me, I wanted to get on the road. It was going to be a long drive to Fort Kent, probably an all-nighter, so I'd unstrapped his canoe, and pulled his beast of an Old Town off the rack with his son Ian's help, and even though we were still 450 miles from Allagash Stream, and Eric stores his canoe upside down to protect it from the elements, true to form, water's magnetic attraction to me demonstrated itself yet again, as I baptize myself with some secret stash of stagnant water, long- sequestered in some canoe cranny; and now my pants, boots and socks gave off a strange stagnant smell that although repugnant to me, seemed to be appreciated by the chickens who couldn't stop pecking at my pant cuffs and boots. I'd been baptized before we'd even packed.

Now it was time for the hurry-up. Feed the chickens, load the truck, throw the canoe on, and head to the closest gas station to fill up and get some truck food; coffee, and junk food, before we hit the road. We stopped at the Kittery Trading Post to supply ourselves with a short list of items, but our timing was a little off and we drove into the parking lot at 9:20 PM, ten minutes before closing. Running in we bowed politely and said; "We know what we need, and we know you want to close we'll get it all done in less than 5 minutes. We ended up with our dehydrated food supplies and a waterproof case for my phone and didn't have time for the new tarp and a couple other things; however, we'd done worse before—although not having a tarp would come back to haunt us on this trip.

After Kittery it was the big drive; all the way to Fort Kent, and then a little more driving to Saint Francis to meet our driver Norm.

Norm brought us up to Peggy's place, we were going to park our truck in her yard for when we returned. We went in; said hi and paid her. "Cash or check" she said, credit and debit cards don't work that well, west of Fort Kent.

Done and gone, we headed for the back woods but not before we stopped at the Allagash Gate and paid the rest of our fees; camping fees, canoeing fees, and possibly some other fees; cash or check, of course, and I was a dollar short. Norm had to cover the shortfall for me, but he didn't seem too concerned. It was a loan and besides he said, "I know where you are."

Heading into the woods on these dirt logging roads, Norman would get on his radio at every mile marker and let people—way out here in the deep woods, know we were coming; "Van passing mile 15." I thought it strange until at mile marker 26 when Norm made his announcement; the radio crackled with a response; "Okay, just ahead and coming your way." Norm pulled the van over just as a very large double-bed, lumber truck doing about 55 miles an hour, came over the rise with a full load of logs swaying back and forth and side to side, while at the same time its tailgate seemed to want to catch up to the front of the truck; organized chaos on this muddy backwater road, and then it was gone. Lumber trucks have the right of way on these private roads, because they "own" these roads. After that it was a comforting thought, when Norm would announce; "Van passing mile 29, or 30, or 31."

I scared a woman half to death right in that seat, said Norm as he pointed to the front passenger seat. I was driving her into the Allagash just like I'm doing with you guys, and she asked me if there were any problems with bears. I told her; "Yes, some, but more with English speaking folks than French speaking." With a look of grave concern, the woman asked why, so I told her; Bears respond to commands better in French than in English. Beginning to look even more upset, I told her not to worry, I could help her by teaching her a few things to say to the bear. I explained that when you see a bear, you should yell Git! "It means the same thing in English as it does in French so the bear should understand what you're saying and go on his way. She was so concerned and serious with trying to get this first lesson down, I had to explain I was only kidding, but I told her if she did run into a bear, Git would be the right thing to yell."

Black bear.

Norman helped us unload our gear, bid us goodbye and good luck, and we pushed off into Allagash Stream, headed towards Round Pond, a great place to see moose. Before we'd paddled more than 100 yards, there it was; not a moose, but the elm, and it was just beginning to show its fall colors. I call it "the elm" because it's probably the most photographed tree in the Maine woods.

There was a time when elm trees were everywhere, and they symbolized significant aspects of community life. There were house elms; single elms that sat in front of many homes, shading and cooling the house against the summer heat; bridal elms, two elms planted together to signify a couples bond in marriage; and defining elms, planted in parks and municipal locations to memorialize a space or event, often taking on the signature of its location: the Harvard Elm, the Springfield Elm, or the Boston Common Elm. And then, there were the streets. Most cities planted elms along their streetscape. An elms shape made it an ideal tree for city streets; growing tall and straight before branching out in umbrella like fashion often meeting elms from the opposite side of the street in the middle, creating a sheltered and shaded canopy. Elm trees were also found sitting alone in a farmer's field. Their stringy, twisted cellular structure makes

elms difficult sometimes to cut down and uncooperative for use for woodworking. It was sometimes just easier to leave the tree standing.

In the early part of the 20th century Dutch Elm disease killed many of the Elm trees in the United States, and Norway maple and other species took their place, but in a few places the American Elm survived. The disease just missed them, and the Allagash is one of those places. Elms flourish in wet environments and the Allagash has larger tracks of Elms that border the Stream, but this particular elm is photographed because of its closeness to the bridge and put-in near Round Pond. It's spectacular because of its shape, and for what it represents; a tree many of us fell in love with, even when we didn't know we had; a subliminal tug is the most powerful of all tugs.

The day was beginning to get hazy. The high thin clouds created just enough of a filter to spread the sunshine around in a glaze that forced a squint for anyone without sunglasses and I had no idea where mine were. Probably in my daypack but I didn't have time to search. I was photographing and scanning the shoreline for any kind of activity.

We were fortunate for the rain the last few days. The upper Allagash is shallow in a lot of places especially in the fall, and the extra water was going to allow us to paddle more, and portage less. We were headed for Cunliffe Depot, the campsite we'd chosen for our first night. Leaving Round Pond there's a set of rapids known as the Round Pond Rips; class I and II but not a big problem, the river was wider than I thought it would be at this point and we were able to angle our canoe into the deepest run. The problem we did run up against a few times was the long flat shallow water runs with just enough water to clear, except you couldn't see the numerous flat boulders that just cleared the surface. We hung up a couple times requiring me to jump out and leverage us off the rock. In deeper water, it was easy to spot the classic vee following a boulder, but some stones didn't exhibit any disturbance in the surface water, and you didn't spot those until you were right on top of them. We didn't have a problem with running into and bouncing off one of these big obstructions. The danger was sliding and catching one sideway with the chance to get hung up and rolled. Rolling the canoe on this trip would have made my capsizing on the Clyde look like a day at the beach. We really didn't want to go there.

We were doing okay running this section and hadn't noticed the change in the color of the sky; it had changed to slate, then gray copper, and now dark. And then the rain came.

There had been a group of three canoes ahead of us for most of the day, and they decided to stop at one of the Deadwater campsites on river left, and we contemplated stopping river right at the Bass Brook campsite but pushed on; we really wanted to get to Cunliffe Depot; that's where the Lombard Log Hauler sat, rusting in the woods.

We barely made it. The last mile was through a field of rips, almost unpaddlable because of its shallowness; we were running in about 10 inches of water. It was also raining hard, torrentially hard, making it hard to even see. I thought at one point we were going to strand and roll in the middle of the river, but we made it, pulling up to our site with just enough energy to secure the boat. We dumped our gear, secured

Round Pond.

Allagash Stream in the fall; a golden time for a canoe trip.

our boat, cooked and ate dinner, and after setting up; me in my single person tent, and Eric in his hammock, we went to bed. It was the best moment of the trip when I crawled in and laid on my bag; pouring outside, it was snug and semi-dry inside. Before I could settle in though I needed to clean my camera gear. Cleaned and secured in their bags, I laid down and started to doze off. I was exhausted and it was only 5:30 p.m.

MORNING

Nothing is simple in the woods. Right now in the morning's pre-dawn light it's raining and I need to find the outhouse, but first I need to find the toilet paper, which is probably stored in one of the waterproof boxes we stacked by the campfire, or since we're camped on a bluff well above the river, it might be in our wannigan; the storage box we have in our canoe, down by the river. After searching it was indeed in the wannigan. and now off I go in the subdued overcast light of morning in search of the little building in the woods. These days, outhouse buildings are kept well away from rivers, ponds, and lakes as a precaution against pollution, making their location sometimes obscure until you do some searching. We hadn't searched yesterday afternoon in the torrential downpour, so I had to search now.

LOMBARD LOG HAULERS

The North Woods in some respects is like a living museum to the logging industry with artifacts sprinkled around in strange places. Some like Chamberlain Farm, have all but disappeared, reclaimed by mother nature, but other still hold vigil, rusting sentinels waiting to be visited by those curious enough to go searching. The largest are the tramway, train engines and box cars left in the woods near Eagle Lake, but equally fascinating are the machines once used for hauling logs in the winter woods. They were known as Lombard log haulers and there are two resting along the Allagash; tucked in the woods, resting where some backwoods logger parked them so many years ago.

From 1900 to 1917, Alvin's factory in Waterville, Maine, produced 83 steam log haulers, but there are only a few in existence today, having long ago served their purpose, most were turned to scrap. The machines ran on steam and pulled log laden sleds through the woods in winter, in preparation for the spring log drives. Lombard's innovative tracked tread system became the prototype for all tanks and other tracked vehicles that followed.

After breakfast we followed the path that led downhill to a small stream, we crossed at a log bridge and continued up the other side, turning toward the woods and after a few yards we saw something curving up out of the ground in the middle of the narrow trail. It was a skid ski, and all of a sudden, we realized just to the left and half covered in foliage was one of the Lombards. It looked like the skeletal remains of some giant beast, and I was awe struck. You just don't see stuff like this hanging around, unless I guess you're in the Allagash. We photographed the beast and continued until we found the second hauler. It was more intact than the first and someone had circled it

Along a short trail behind the Cunliffe Depot campsite, you can find two Lombard Log Haulers, sitting were they were parked sometime in the 1930s; these machines were used to pull sleds full of logs to the riverbanks to await the spring ice-out. One of these metal ghosts is a steam hauler, the other ran on gasoline. Both of these haunted remains are over 110 years old and have been sitting in their present location for the past ninety.

with an old snow fence; probably because of the asbestos sheeting that we could see spilling from the bottom of the boiler. It was an impressive site. There were also parts of things scattered around, the weirdest one as far as I was concerned was the metal bucket hanging off the side. How long has that thing been sitting there?

It was time to get moving, so we headed back, broke camp, loaded up and headed downriver. We were on our way to the ranger station at Michaud Farm.

When the farm was in sight, we could see three canoes tucked up on the small shingle and I could hear someone talking. I recognized his French-Canadian accent when I heard him say; "Hey, those are my photographers." It was Norman, and he yelled across to us to let us know we didn't need to sign in; the book was full, so we continued on downstream, but not before I yelled back to tell Norm I didn't have his dollar yet.

We were now headed for Allagash falls, and the portage around the falls isn't something you want to miss. The drop is only 40 feet, but it looks like 400 when you view it from the bottom. Portaging took a couple hours and while we were moving our

stuff, the group of three canoes arrived and much to my surprise it was someone I knew. Polly who runs Mahoosuc Guide Service was guiding a group down the river. Polly and I had met a few years earlier when I was working on a book and needed to photograph some dogsledding, something else Mahoosuc offers. We had a problem with scheduling and a snow problem, but we'd made a connection and it was great to see her again.

For those who want to experience the Allagash but don't feel they have the skill-set to go it alone, they can paddle the Allagash on a guided trip with a registered Maine Guide like my friend Polly. The Mahoosuc Guide Service is one of the most respected and experienced recreational guide services in New England, and they have canoeing options for any level including those with no experience. They've been running guided trips for over 27 years with great success. If you contact Polly, tell them, Dan sent you.

Portage time.

PORTAGE
ALL PARTIES
MUST CARRY

The Saint John River on its
way to Fort Kent.

Polly and her group were camping at Allagash Falls for the night, but Eric and I were headed downstream to Big Brook East where we spent the evening. The rain had stopped but everything was still wet and our attempt at a campfire was marginally successful, but we did have one. The following day we ran the rest of the river on water that was easier than anticipated. The water level had risen again and many of the dangerous section of rapids and rips were faster but less obstructed. We flew down the river, arriving at Allagash Village and Peggy's house ahead of schedule. Eric went to find the keys and bring the truck down to the water's edge while I sat and reflected on what we'd accomplished. It was a great trip and a great journey for the both of us. We were both still soaking wet and didn't have any dry clothes but that wasn't a big deal at that point. We could always find some dry clothes once we got back to Fort Kent, if not maybe we could find a Walmart. First though, I needed to go to Pelletier's Campground and give Norman the dollar I owed him.

End of the line until next year.

Allagash Falls.